# THE BERNAL STORY

Syracuse Studies in Peace and Conflict Resolution

Robert A. Rubinstein, *Series Editor*

Other titles from Syracuse Studies on Peace and Conflict Resolution

# The
# BERNAL
## Story

. . .

*Mediating Class and Race
in a Multicultural Community*

. . .

## Beth Roy

Foreword by John Paul Lederach

Syracuse University Press

First Edition 2014
14  15  16  17  18  19       6  5  4  3  2  1

∞ The paper used in this publication meets the minimum requirements of
the American National Standard for Information Sciences—Permanence of
Paper for Printed Library Materials, ANSI Z39.48-1992.

For a listing of books published and distributed by Syracuse University Press,
visit www.SyracuseUniversityPress.syr.edu.

ISBN: 978-0-8156-3346-4 (cloth)       978-0-8156-5276-2 (e-book)

**Library of Congress Cataloging-in-Publication Data**
Roy, Beth.
   The Bernal story : mediating class and race in a multicultural community /
Beth Roy ; foreword by John Paul Lederac. — First edition.
      pages cm. — (Syracuse studies in peace and conflict resolution)
   Includes bibliographical references and index.
   ISBN 978-0-8156-3346-4 (cloth : alk. paper) — ISBN 978-0-8156-5276-2
(ebook) 1. Bernal Heights (San Francisco, Calif.)  2. Community development—
California—San Francisco.  3. Community life—California—San Francisco.
4. Intergroup relations—California—San Francisco.  5. Culture conflict—
California—San Francisco.  6. Conflict management—California—San Francisco.
7. Bernal Heights (San Francisco, Calif.)—Ethnic relations.  I. Title.
   HN80.S4R69 2014
   307.1'40979461—dc23                                          2014014001

*Manufactured in the United States of America*

## A Note on Confidentiality

*The Bernal Story* recounts an extraordinary effort by neighbors to work through searing conflict in a diverse community. Not the least of the contributions the group made was its willingness to support this account of its process. When I asked whether people were willing for me to write the book and, further, whether they sought anonymity or preferred to appear in their true identities, every individual gave clear and eager consent to waive confidentiality. That decision is courageous and generous, and a testament to the process they undertook: the Bernal mediation group knows itself to have engaged in respectful dialogue with utmost honesty. Its story therefore casts nothing but honor on those who took part.

**Beth Roy**, PhD, is a longtime mediator in the San Francisco Bay Area. Trained as a sociologist at University of California, Berkeley, she teaches there in the Peace and Conflict Studies program. She writes books on social conflict, most recently *41 Shots . . . and Counting: What Amadou Diallo Teaches Us about Policing, Race, and Justice* (Syracuse University Press, 2008). Dr. Roy is a founder of the Practitioners Research and Scholarship Institute (PRASI), a network of conflict resolution practitioners dedicated to supporting colleagues whose cultures and approaches were absent from the existing literature to regard their lived experience as the basis of research and to write their knowledge for publication. She coedited *Re-Centering Culture and Knowledge in Conflict Resolution Practice* (Syracuse University Press, 2008).

# Contents

# Illustrations

# Foreword

AS WE HAVE COME TO EXPECT from Beth Roy, *The Bernal Story* is a gift to the practice of mediation and the wider domain of peacebuilding. I say *as we have come to expect from Beth* because her work represents a rarity within our literature. She combines the *best practices* of astute ethnography with the *best scholarship* arising from experienced and lived practice.

The insights emerging from the description and analysis unraveled in this book speak to so many of our contemporary local and global conflicts. We live in worlds that challenge our imagination. I refer to *worlds* in plural to emphasize the simultaneous nature of local communities that make up daily life, and the global realities we share transnationally where we must find ways to create dynamic and responsive communities from the gristmill of tangled human relationships that too often rage into destructive patterns of conflict.

Having just celebrated Martin Luther King Jr.'s fiftieth anniversary of the walk on Washington and his iconic *I Have a Dream* speech, I would argue that in large part, *The Bernal Story* points us toward practical and engaged ways the beloved community emerges. At the most fundamental level, the Bernal community mediation process generated much more than mediation, and yet rooted its growth in simple truths: relationships that matter require sufficient safety to allow honest and iterative communication to deepen toward understanding. Safety begins with recovery of social and personal dignity, things we need and can protect for and with each other even when we have deep differences and come from significantly divergent identities and lived experience.

Let there be no mistake: the challenges of constructive change portrayed in these pages move toward and into the more difficult aspects of conflict that mediation techniques cannot and should not blithely remove. How do we engage and stay with relationships when power and identity bump heads and in contexts where exclusion and privilege speak loudly and silently at the same time? Beth's approach, outlined in this rich narrative description and thorough analysis, moves into the heart of these matters and does so with the full participation of the community. I would highlight several gifts embedded in this story that stood out to me in large part because they resonated deeply with my own experience and practice.

First, in *The Bernal Story* we find an extraordinary *ethnography of process*, of how dialogue actually emerged and was nurtured. Much of our literature relies on "cases," as if they are just that: anecdotal examples. Here we find ourselves accompanying the unfolding of a community narrative replete with the full humanity—real people with their concerns and lives, and most importantly, their participation. This story has every element of the *elicitive approach* that departs from the premise that people have experience, knowledge, understanding, and capacity to name and respond to the very realities they create. We find no mention of "The Parties" in conflict; instead, we enter the lives, discourse, and the very act of making meaning pursued by Darcy and Dan, and Mauricio and Susan, to mention just a few.

Second, we find here a *reflective ethnography* of a mediator in situ, that is, of a person engaged with the community and who intriguingly knows neighbors, has friends, and hails from and is still connected to the community she writes about. Having multiple roles and multiplicities of crosscutting relationships, Beth exemplifies an embedded facilitator pursuing dialogue that requires constant innovation while navigating her role, relationships, and contribution. As she describes in her conclusion, *The Bernal Story* defies narrow notions of neutrality and suggests that we as professionals widen our capacity to come alongside social change in ways that require innovation of roles and a fluid dynamic that seeks to fill a range of needs, functions, and support in social change processes.

Third, this story reflects a refreshing honesty of discourse and ideas. Moving toward and into the challenges of power and identity, love and justice, and in contexts of deep social and racial division requires that we locate and nourish a platform of honest and sustained relational engagement. This story provides many clues about how honesty—with self and other—emergent in trusted spaces will always trump social and political correctness.

Finally, *The Bernal Story* tells us that dialogue takes time. It will not happen in short sessions pieced together in order to attain an agreement. The story has specific suggestions about approach and technique, but those are never valued over the hard work of fully exploring and preparing the terrain, developing participatory avenues by which process is defined and perceptions unpacked, and the basic commitment to relationships.

This is the beloved community—one that does not fear a conversation about tough issues and deep differences, and one that commits to remaining engaged with each other even when the going is slow and tough. For the thick description we receive in this book and the insights borne from the process, I am grateful. *The Bernal Story* suggests that hope for constructive social change in response to deep identity divides in this country has a strong grounding in empirical evidence, and it challenges us to both widen and deepen our practices of facilitated meaningful and responsive conversation.

John Paul Lederach
September 10, 2013

# Part One

. . .

*The Story of a Well-Fought Conflict*

# 1

# The Context

## *Exploring the Terrain*

SAN FRANCISCO is a city of hills and water, of culture and political activism, of charm and innovation—and of conflict. Early in the twenty-first century, all those elements combined in one lovely neighborhood called Bernal Heights. The city's branch public libraries were slated for renovation, a generous and welcome thing that nonetheless had generated heated controversy in Bernal. On the walls of the Bernal library, a mural, originally colorful but now faded and flaking, inflamed passions: some neighbors identified strongly with the images and were determined to have them restored, while another group insisted that the walls be unadorned, returned to the original intention of the building's architect.

The Bernal community is capable of storming badly when passionate opinions and tempers flare. The Bernal community also regards itself as an exemplar of social values, a place committed to equity and justice. The library mural controversy, therefore, challenged the neighborhood's self-image: the feud, raging over eight years, became increasingly vitriolic. Commission meetings were torn apart by name-calling, celebratory moments marred by sloganeering. Factions organized and maligned each other in public forums.

Finally, a month before the library was to reopen, a small group of leaders came forward to try to restore civility. Therein began a story of mediation, creative collaboration, and social growth. Much was learned along the way, and the participants in the process now offer to share those lessons.

*3*

■   ■   ■

San Francisco is a city of discrete neighborhoods. Geographically defined by hills and water, each district has its own shopping area, and each is associated with particular qualities and cultures. The Mission District, or "The Mission," has traditionally been known as the heart of Spanish-speaking San Francisco; The Castro for its gay residents. The Haight-Ashbury, famed for its centrality to the flower-child phenomenon of the 1960s, has had varied identities over the decades; today it is hip, often compared to Manhattan's Greenwich Village. Valencia Street, meanwhile, is the city's Soho, a corridor rich with avant-garde galleries and experimental theatres. Valencia divides The Mission from Noe Valley, a neighborhood that was once working-class white Catholic and today has become upscale, expensive, and filled with young families. The Bayview to the south is predominantly black, a spirited community laced with long-standing civic, cultural, and advocacy organizations.

Similarly, Bernal Heights has a history and a culture all its own. Bridging The Mission and The Bayview, stretching across a treeless peak to the industrial Bayshore on the east, Bernal was historically noted for three qualities: multiculturalism, progressive values, and earthquake bungalows. With a history stretching back to farming, the community grew rapidly after the 1906 earthquake. Hills are prized in seismically active country, for they offer the possibility of anchoring buildings into stable bedrock. When the "big one" rocked the Bay Area early in the twentieth century, ingenious prefab shacks were quickly built and set up, row after row, in the city's parks. Intended to be temporary housing—an improvement on the flimsier tents that were first supplied—some citizens carted off the tiny one-room houses to plant them in seismically secure parts of the city. Many found their way to the rocky heights of Bernal hill, where they were loved and often expanded over the years. These small homes invited a working-class population. As immigration expanded the density of the Mission District, Bernal's demography also became increasingly diverse. Spanish speakers from Mexico and Central America lived side-by-side with white blue-collar families and Filipino and Chinese newcomers.

By the turn of the twentieth century, San Francisco's harbor had become central to the city's political culture, defined by an alliance of two forces: leftist trade unionists, most centrally in the Longshoreman's Union, and progressive European immigrants who built fortunes and used them to sponsor the cultural life of the city. In 1934, as part of a campaign to organize seamen, a city-wide general strike—one of only two in the history of the United States—took place.

Over the years, Bernal became a locus of activists, attracted by its affordability and increasingly its values and cultures. White working-class people occupying the small bungalows of the community were joined over the decades by newcomers from Mexico and Central America. Latino Bernalites related to the larger Mission District, but also saw themselves as a distinct community within Bernal. A sizeable settling of people from the Philippines joined the mix. Reasonably cordial relations existed among the various ethnic groups, although interaction was typically limited. As time went by, the neighborhood had its economic ups and downs and concomitant social tensions. By the 1970s its central street, Cortland Avenue, had become shabby. Gang activities made the shopping area a place with a hazardous reputation. Graffiti marked youth territories. In 1978 a progressive community organization was formed: the Bernal Heights Neighborhood Center (BHNC) declared its mission to improve the neighborhood in terms of both social relations and resources, and also to protect its accessibility to people of modest means. It succeeded in building a series of affordable housing projects around the hill, as well as launching social programs for the community: among others, activities for seniors and projects for youths intended to build nonviolent relations.

But gradually the rising economic tides of San Francisco lapped against the boundaries of Bernal. As Silicon Valley grew to the south, so too did the cost of housing in the city to its north. Bernal was relatively late in gentrifying, but eventually its southern location, so convenient to the commute to the dot-com industry mushrooming a few miles away, combined with its village demeanor, made the neighborhood a desirable home site for newly-affluent young families. Bernal became a hill divided. Property values on the northwest slope escalated first, followed to a lesser extent by other sections. The BHNC did its best to support amicable community relations, but conflict simmered, and now and then burst through.

## Books and Art

There are two other elements that characterize each San Francisco neighborhood: branch libraries and particular styles of public art. San Franciscans make good use of their libraries; the librarians provide rich programs for young people and appealing access for adults. In 2002, the electorate approved a generous bond measure to renovate every one of the nine branch libraries. Work proceeded slowly over the years; by the time the Bernal Library was closed for renovation, the economic winds had blown in hard times, so the gorgeously-designed reclamation of the building stood in contrast to tight program budgets. For some members of the community, the physical structure of the library holds special meaning. It was built as an outgrowth of community activism; in 1936, despite privations of the Depression, neighbors lobbied for a new library. Work Projects Administration (or WPA) funds were secured and a well-respected architect, Frederick H. Meyer, contracted to design it. The library, a sweet one-story structure, with columns framing a staircase to an impressive entrance, opened in October 1940. Still today, the building stands as one of the few structures in Bernal considered architecturally significant.

Meanwhile, the Bernal library exemplified a particular kind of art, as well. In the early 1980s a mural had been painted on three of its facades. Street murals hold a special kind of meaning in San Francisco. In a tribute to the important place of Mexican culture in the city, people of Latin heritage have spearheaded a movement called "muralissimo" that is joined and appreciated across ethnic boundaries. Throughout The Mission, and today throughout much of the city, buildings both private and public are adorned with elaborate and imaginative paintings. Many of these works reflect a specifically Mexican style, telling stories of oppression and heroism in vivid colors and images. Whole alleys are taken as public palettes for expression of community sentiments. Other works are more decorative, relating to a particular place or site.

Mural art on city walls is cousin to another form of artistic expression: graffiti. By the late 1970s, Bernal's central commercial street, Cortland Avenue, had become a bleak stretch of closed shops, storefront law firms, and small food shops. Young people had contributed lots and lots of graffiti, the library being a prime target for their creative talents. In the summer of 1980, a San Francisco muralist, Arch Williams, with the support of the neighborhood center, obtained some city funds to do an anti-graffiti, youth-employment project at the library. The project stretched over four years, resulting in artwork that wrapped around the building. The south wall told the story of Bernal, starting with a large depiction of a native-American couple and a well-antlered deer. Beneath this foundational image the young people painted scenes of the neighborhood, including the hill itself, Cortland Avenue shops, working people, bicyclists, and a well-groomed red car, a 1937 Plymouth "bomb" dear to the hearts of many of the young painters.

During the time the work progressed, a young Filipino man from the neighborhood was killed, a victim of gang violence. The muralists painted a moving memorial to him on the west wall, embedded in dramatic images of unity and peace: in the center of a stylized sun were two clasped hands, one brown, the other black, extending from rays that rose above images of four working women of diverse ethnicities, ages, and activities, surrounding a portrait of the slain youth.

The primary themes of the front façade facing Cortland Avenue were song, social justice, and the future. A figure adorned the left side, looking skyward and seeming to release four birds, painted in diverse cultural styles, toward a rainbow. Words from a song written by Holly Near, a popular feminist performer at the time, rose from the figure. On the right was another figure, facing toward the street and holding a guitar. This image was not clearly identified, but the words above its head were from a song by Victor Jara, a young activist Chilean poet and singer who was murdered in 1973 by the Augusto Pinochet dictatorship. Above his head were the words of his song: "Tu canto es rio, sol y viento, pajaro que anuncia la paz. Your song is the river, the sun and wind, a bird announcing peace."

The main entrance to the building divided the "song" portion of the mural from the future: a series of pyramids in varied cultural styles and a rising curl of blue that became background for a series of globes and galaxies receding into the distance of the universe.

This schema had been designed and implemented under the supervision of a practiced muralist, but with intensive input from many community residents. The youths were paid small stipends to paint; some of them were inspired to become muralists and community artists themselves.

While art on public buildings is a grand tradition in San Francisco, this particular art and this building were at war with each other. Advocates of the building cited its architecture, WPA history, and importance to the neighborhood to argue for restoration of its walls to their original, unadorned cream color. Devotees of the artwork claimed it as cultural heritage, passionately arguing that its erasure would be another harm done to poorer and older residents who had increasingly been forced by escalating property values to cling precariously to their homes or move to the poorer southern suburbs.

**The Immediate Dispute**

Battles that are properly defined as political often take place on cultural terrain. In an earlier work, I considered the ways in which culture becomes a means of mobilizing people of like identity to fight for resources and rights (Roy 1994). If there appear to be no other roads toward well-being, people will come together around what they believe to be their tightest bonds with others. Religious identity, language, race, and locality all offer a framework within which people can write stories of shared interests. Sometimes, culture and politics are so closely knit together in these processes as to become inseparable. Just so in Bernal, a conflict based in class differences was fought out by disputing the fate of a cultural artifact. As residents of lesser means found themselves upended by newcomers who were more affluent, they sought a language in which to stand up for their place in the community. Many people who were not Latino found themselves in an identical plight. Bernal had long been a white working-class neighborhood, including many women homeowners, single and lesbian, who could afford property on the hill but not elsewhere in the city. These neighbors, too, were losing their footing in a community in which they were invested. The local neighborhood center had provided some voice for resisting change, but the economy, powerfully fueled by the new technological industries just south of the city, overwhelmed these efforts.

And so, when the library mural became threatened, some long-term residents of Latino heritage invoked that identity to defend an artistic artifact embedded in a cultural tradition that was widely associated with Latin culture. As the story unfolded, these themes of identity, culture, and politics animated the drama, contributing a great deal of passion and a patina of intractability.

By January 2010, when the library was scheduled to reopen, city authorities were desperate for a solution. Commission meetings had been weighted with vituperative exchanges, ceremonial occasions disrupted by angry protests. Solutions proposed by city authorities only led to intensified hostilities, satisfying no one and at the same time increasing suspicions that one side or the other enjoyed privileged status.

Just before Christmas, 2009, Bernal Heights' elected representative to city government, known as a supervisor, together with the executive director of the neighborhood center approached me to mediate the conflict.

### To Mediate or Not to Mediate?

At that point, I had lived in Bernal for sixteen years—making me a newcomer. I operated a counseling and conflict resolution practice out of my sweet bungalow home. Many of my clients were neighbors, and this being Bernal, many of my neighbors were friends. Darcy Lee, an individual in all three categories, had put forward my name; she headed the local association of merchants, and she had become a

central figure in the controversy. Over the years I've gained a reputation for working on heated dynamics of race and ethnicity. In my
practice of mediation and also my research into social conflict, I've
focused on themes of power, emotion, and social justice. That background suggested to the community leadership that I might be able
to do something to address the library tempest.

From the very beginning, therefore, I did not appear in the
story as a neutral professional. I did not have distance from the people involved, nor were my views on many of the underlying issues
unknown. It was true that I had not taken a position about the dispute
itself; indeed, I had no particular opinion. I had always been charmed
by the mural, and I also respected the aesthetic acumen of some of
the people lobbying for clean walls. But I was dismayed by much of
what I was hearing—words of disrespect hurled back and forth with
seemingly little regard for the principles of right treatment I thought
characterized my neighborhood and had attracted me to live here in
the first place.

So I agreed to meet with Supervisor David Campos, Executive
Director Joseph Smooke, a staff person named Rachel Ebora (who
soon after succeeded Joseph as director), and a board member from
the center. The latter was Larry Cruz, a well-loved elder in the city.
Earlier, he had facilitated some community meetings that had turned
painful, despite his best leadership efforts. I didn't know Larry,
but it turned out he lived only a few doors away from me. Latino
and gay, a longtime homeowner, he uniquely commanded respect
across the spectrum of controversies by dint of wisdom, humor, and
good-heartedness.

We met one early morning over coffee at a local café. Supervisor
Campos and Director Smooke laid out their appeal for help. Another
community meeting co-chaired by Larry and me was mentioned by
someone, and Larry quickly demurred. "No more public meetings!"
he avowed. The others agreed that there had been ample opportunity
for both individuals and organized citizens' groups to air their feelings and positions. Now, something more was needed, something that

would address the divisions and bring about a shift in the tenor of the discourse.

My approach to mediation has been labeled many things: both transformational and directive, relationship- and settlement-oriented, elicitive and structured. To me, all those labels justly apply. The work is elicitive in the sense of John Paul Lederach's (1997) invention of the term. John Paul is a Mennonite luminary, a talented intervener in society-level conflicts. When he is called to a Latin American or an African land where conflict is afoot, he begins by listening closely to the feelings, cultures, and needs of the people involved, deriving a form for the work as it arises from those discussions. In that sense, the structure of an intervention is elicited by the cultures and the conflicts at hand. John Paul's approach is based in a philosophy concerning power relations. By encouraging the participants in a conflict to design an intervention culturally appropriate to themselves, John Paul underscores the fundamental premise of mediation, that the process belongs to the people involved. Elicitive intervention thus practices from the beginning what many other approaches may preach but contradict with long lists of ground rules and structural imperatives.

My own approach is similarly cognizant of the dynamics of power distribution, but there is a catch that also concerns me. Usually by the time conflict is "ripe" for intervention, a lot of pain has been experienced. People are often discouraged, depleted, and deeply alienated from each other. While empowerment is needed, so too is leadership. Balancing those two convictions—that the parties to a conflict are the heart and soul of its solution, and that leadership offering new hope and new ideas is equally needed—is where conflict transformation (to use Lederach's language) becomes an art form rather than a protocol. I believe that form and function cannot be disentwined. When I work with a family or a small group in a familiar social setting, I offer a structure—with flexibility. I advise participants in advance to prepare for a mediation session, posing a series of questions and offering a set of tools. I also speak with them beforehand and listen to a short version of their story. If that dialogue suggests that something unique to their situation would be more helpful, I construct that guidance in consultation with them. Sometimes, a few minutes into a session are enough to convince me a redesign is needed. Structure, in other words, must follow reality; the map is not the territory, but it is a useful guide.

## Designing a Community Intervention

A situation like the Bernal case, however, is a lot more complex. At that café table, John Paul was more in my mind than my standard format. The first question to address was very basic: Who should be involved? At a public forum, participants select themselves—anyone can come. To be sure, a good organizer might reach out to certain groups or individuals to ensure that a meaningful dialogue can take place. In this regard, roles of facilitator and of organizer overlap. I believed that any group convened to address the Bernal controversy would need to be small enough for genuinely constructive dialogue to take place. At the same time, it needed to reflect as wide a variety of viewpoints as possible. A third requirement was that the individuals physically at the table would need to be influential in their particular circles, otherwise the work we would be doing might help transform relationships among a small group of people, but that would have only limited impact on the community as a whole. Each individual participant would have to bring to the process openness to change, a commanding voice, and willingness to energetically engage and influence neighbors who were not present for the work. Those were large requirements, but I suspected they could be fulfilled. That confidence was built on the unique opportunity I'd enjoyed over several decades of doing this work to see human beings at their best. Conflict is all about change; when skills for pursuing conflict are in short supply, as they mostly are, change can loom as a frightening prospect, something to be avoided or resisted. But constructively handled, conflict can produce an eagerness to understand its causes and embark on new directions informed by the insights gained. I knew from my own life in the neighborhood that commanding voices would be in no short supply. I also knew that when community conflict is afoot, people tend to huddle with like-minded folks. I felt sure there would be identifiable opinion circles and that they would constitute complex social networks. I was also sure that not everyone would fit neatly into categories, sharing homogenously either social identities or positions in the dispute at hand. It would be necessary to identify advocates of the major positions, and equally to identify those who had not spoken out publically because they either disdained the vituperative discourse or held more nuanced opinions.

Already, sipping coffee with my fellow planners, the sociologist in me was excited. The mediator, however, was anxious. I began to sketch out my thoughts, starting with two caveats: First, I wasn't yet convinced I was the right mediator for the job. So far, the controversy had appeared to have two racially-identified sides: Latino residents wanting to save the mural, and white residents wanting it gone. I was pretty sure that that broad-stroke description—based on nothing more than theory—was inadequate, but I equally believed it had some kernels of truth and therefore a good deal of power in terms of public perception. I've mediated multicultural disputes for many years, and in the process I've been privileged to learn a good deal about the perspectives of peoples whose cultures I do not share. But I know enough to know that there's a lot that I don't and can't know. My preference, therefore, is always to work with co-mediators who have more first-hand knowledge of the pieces I know less well. I was reassured that Larry would work closely with me. In addition, my mind was already scanning lists of colleagues, wondering who might be available to join the work on the Bernal project.

If I did mediate, then the second immediate consideration or caveat needed to be stated right away: What exactly was the objective of this project? I did not want to hold out promise of settling the issue. The dispute itself was a classic example of a zero-sum conflict. There was one primary wall of the library, the one facing Cortland Avenue. The polarized positions were irreconcilable: the wall could either be blank or adorned, not both. I knew that compromises—painting other walls with murals, putting artwork on only part of the Cortland façade—had already been roundly rejected by one side or the other. So I believed that the chances of coming up with a "third way" were very, very slim. I would not undertake to lead a process that I suspected had so little chance of success.

What I tentatively proposed was that I work toward a process intended to restore good relations within the community. I thought we could help people clear the emotional air, generating a shared set of principles for disagreeing more constructively. When a small group of people learns to conduct controversy in a respectful way, the influence of that spirit can expand outward to a larger community. That was my sense of a goal for the work.

Conflict intervention approaches can be arrayed on a range from relational to settlement focused. On the relational end, the goal of the work is to engage deeper understanding of divergent points of view, opening channels of compassion and promoting ways of conducting respectful disagreement. On the settlement side of the spectrum, the goal is to bring the dispute to a conclusion satisfactory to all participants. What distinguishes mediation from other forms of adjudication is that the solution arises from the disputants itself, rather than being imposed by an outside force. In that sense, all mediation relies to some extent on a shift in relationship. But not all mediation brings about a positive shift; sometimes compromises are constructed that allow people to let go of fixed positions, but not necessarily leading them to like each other any better.

What I was proposing for Bernal was very much on the relational end of the spectrum. I knew that the outcome would be limited in that one side or the other was likely to "lose" and would have to come to terms with not getting what they wanted. My hope was to open pathways so that conclusion might happen with good grace born of deepened understanding of the other side's perspective.

Mediators are not supposed to bring their own interests to the table. I did have an agenda, though. Understanding that the deep underlying issues of this conflict were about race, culture, and class, I had an analysis of the dynamics that was born of my work over the years, both in practice and through research. I fully expected to see some of these dynamics playing out here. While I was prepared to learn a whole lot more as the work proceeded about just how they were playing out, I also believed that the process would allow for consciousness raising along the way. That process is very close to my heart; it reflects my own values and politics, and I forthrightly stated my interest to the small group with whom I was meeting.

They were equally honest in telling me there was no money available to pay me. They thought they could raise some funds along the way, but there were no guarantees. The matter of money raised some delicate questions. Was I entering the arena as a neighbor or as a paid professional? How would one or the other identity shape my reception? How, indeed, would they influence my actions and the outcomes of the whole undertaking? Uncharacteristically, I was willing to let the questions play out as we went along. Normally, it's important to have the material conditions of mediating clearly specified from the start. In truth, I wanted to be paid something, because I was bringing to the work professional skills gained through many years of experience. Money also connotes a certain authority; payment to some extent is a means to negotiate power relations. It gives to the "professional" the power to act in particular ways.

On the other hand, I didn't really care how much I would be paid, or in the final event whether I would be at all. To mediate the Bernal conflict seemed as natural an act as stepping out my front door in the morning and greeting a neighbor. This was my community, and the underlying tensions that were inflamed at the moment mattered dearly to me. I believed that the work we were agreeing to undertake together would be sufficiently compelling and helpful that people would accord me whatever authority I needed to lead them. I also sensed I would learn a lot, a special treat after four decades of practice. I could rely on at least that much compensation.[1]

And so we agreed: onward!

---

1. In the end, many months later, various sources contributed to an honorarium of $3,000 for the mediation. I did, indeed, feel honored.

## Who Sits at the Table?

We set about to create a list of names. Who were the apparent leaders of the controversy? Some were obvious: the president of the Bernal merchants' association, the director of a locally-based community arts program, the president of the neighborhood center's board, one of the branch librarians. My notes for the meeting included one more name, with a big question mark after it: "Mauricio?"

I knew Mauricio Vela's name and had met him once or twice when he was running for school board or the board of supervisors, races he had not won but which had gained him a city-wide reputation. He was also a past director of the neighborhood center. I knew he had been hired and mentored by a good friend of mine, Helen Helfer, who had for many years directed the center. Helen now was retired and lived on the east coast, but I remembered her speaking of Mauricio with respect and affection.

What I thought I was hearing at the café, though, was a signifi-cant amount of trepidation. As we talked, I learned that Mauricio was the organizer of a group called "Save the Bernal Library Mural." He had mounted a noisy campaign, organizing present and past residents to demonstrate at library events and testify at commission hearings. Nobody spoke disrespectfully of him that morning, but they debated whether he would agree to mediation, or whether he even could be mediated. He was a firebrand, passionately dedicated to his commu-nity and to his position. They were doubtful that he would recognize grounds for any sort of mediated solution.

On the other hand, they also questioned whether a mediation without Mauricio would accomplish anything. Any "resolution" that left Mauricio out was sure to perpetuate the current discord, perhaps even to further inflame it. I asked that his contact information be included in the data they promised to send me so that I could explore those questions directly with him.

The question of who should participate in a mediation becomes increasingly complex as the scope of the dispute increases. In fact, I believe it is almost always useful to give the matter detailed thought, even when it seems clear who should be present. In the United States, our approach to conflict intervention is heavily influenced by both legal and therapeutic models. Confidentiality precludes an expansive reading of who might helpfully be present. In a divorce matter, only the married partners are involved, but what about the in-laws, the grown children, the ministers and others who are affected by the outcome? I had the privilege of participating in conflict resolution work in rural Bangladesh. In one case, neighbors were complaining about frequent fights between a couple. It was clear that the man was physically mistreating his wife. The mediators, respected leaders of a local NGO, leaned heavily on him to take part in mediation. About eighty people crowded into the room, many of them telling stories of what they'd heard and said and how they felt about the drama. In the end, with a little gentle persuasion from the NGO director, who threatened to withhold resources if the beatings continued, the man agreed to forego violence. I recognize that this example contains a large element of social control. Provocatively, I would argue that even the most even-handed, professionally neutral mediator brings with her assumptions and biases, however overt or unexpressed, that influence the process she leads. "Control" may be weak, but it nonetheless shades every professional encounter. The role of "mediator" intrinsically carries with it a set of cultural values: it is better to collaborate than to fight; reason is superior to emotion; individual autonomy is possible to achieve and necessary for collaborative decision-making. Collectivism in South Asia produces a very different process from what we conduct in the United States under assumptions of individualism. Participants' processes cannot but be influenced by that which is unspoken at least as much as by what is openly stated.

I was, therefore, very conscious that our choices of participants to take part in an intervention would form a very particular cultural and conceptual structure within which to work. At the public forums that had so far occurred, two positions were loudly advocated: exact restoration of the existing mural, and complete removal of the mural. The Cortland façade was especially contentious, for it was considered by everyone to be the public face of the community. Judging by my own earlier passivity in the dispute, I guessed that there were many other residents who either took no position or had ideas that had not been expressed. My plan was to talk with as many involved members of the community as I could in the next few weeks, to map the breadth of the controversy in an attempt to select a group that was as representative of the community as possible both demographically and in terms of perspectives on the issue at hand.

This stage in designing the approach was again influenced by John Paul Lederach. His work in divided societies has led him to define three categories of those who need to be involved in interventions: official leaders, grassroots people, and a middle stratum of those who are held in esteem in the course of everyday interactions. He calls these groups top leadership, middle-range leadership, and grassroots leadership (Lederach 1997, 41). My aim was first to identify people who fit the middle description, then to expand to the third one. I thought the requirement for "top leadership" involvement would be fulfilled by David, our very powerfully involved elected representative.

But unlike John Paul's elicitive approach to finding and recruiting participants, I quickly realized I needed to be a good deal more directive. Any model for intervention needs to be fitted to the given circumstances. We had a very short timeline: the café meeting took place in late December; the library was scheduled to reopen on January 30. The city leaders had a fear that the ceremonies might be disrupted and a commensurately strong desire that some intervention head off any such public protest. Working with Larry, I set about to make the choice of participants myself, in consultation with many others, but with the final power and the final responsibility resting clearly with me. To have done something more democratic, I thought, would put the cart before the horse, risking inflaming divisions in the course of trying to construct a process for allaying those very same divisions. In other circumstances, my inclinations are very much collaborative, but this time I sensed a need for decisive leadership.

# 2

# The Setup

## *Composition and Design*

I BEGAN by contacting the people on Supervisor Campos and Director Smooke's short list. The first to respond was a librarian working at our branch. She offered me a tour, even though renovation was still in progress. As we walked through the building, her excitement mounted each time I praised what I saw. The building was wonderful. Wooden tables had been restored to their original grandeur. The ceiling was stenciled with designs. Grand lighting fixtures had been reconstructed according to images from the past. The lower level of the building—in the past, a dank storage area that had also for a time housed a nursery school—had been turned into a glorious children's library and a room for community meetings.

When we circled the exterior, the librarian's tone shifted; she made no secret of her hope that the mural would be gone. She disliked it aesthetically and disapproved of it architecturally. We talked about the pros and cons of librarians participating in the mediation; she expressed strong reservations. As a library employee, her role would be very different from everyone else's. Moreover, she dealt with the public on a daily basis and heard people's strong feelings, pro and con the mural. She felt it was appropriate to her position to let the community served by the library make the decision. I later spoke with the city librarian who concurred that staff participation was too troubled an arrangement. But I asked my librarian-tour guide to send me names of people she thought I should consult, and almost before

I had traveled the few blocks to my home her message arrived in my in-box with a thorough list.

In short order, I spoke with Johanna Silva Waki, the chair of the Bernal Heights Neighborhood Center's board, who warmed my heart by immediately identifying a need to talk honestly about hurt feelings; Susan Cervantes, the director of a local mural organization, who told me of her concern that losing the Bernal mural would impact the ability of muralists all over the city to get funding; Darcy Lee, the president of the Bernal merchants' organization, who had drawn a good deal of anger by sponsoring a petition urging the erasure of the mural and was now enthusiastic about mediating the issue.

I was still concerned and eager to partner with a colleague who could better reflect the culture about which I know less. When Larry Cruz had been proposed as that person, he telegraphed his discomfort. The more the mediation took shape, the more Larry demurred. Now retired, and a Bernal homeowner for many years, Larry had spent his career working for the city in a variety of positions, including deputy mayor. He knew a great deal about dynamics of public controversy. Wise, skilled, and experienced as he was, he had never led a process like this one, and while he was eager to learn more skills, he was pretty sure he didn't want to jump into the deep water. All the more for his honest reluctance, I knew I wanted him involved. So we renegotiated his role, settling on his taking part as a participant at the same time that he continued to consult with me as I explored circles of residents on the hill.

I set about to find another co-mediator. There was a young woman living in southern California, originally from Mexico City, with whom I'd worked in the past; I greatly respected her. She had trained with me for some time, and we continued to consult as her cross-national practice developed. I called Cynthia Luna and asked if she might be available to co-mediate a first session. She readily agreed, although we realized that I would need to do a greater share of the pre-meeting work, since I was local and she was scheduled to be in Mexico over the next several weeks. In our initial conversation, she made two interconnected, crucial points. People were arguing about history, she noted, but not really talking about it. And when people with roots in Mexico and South America talk about history, the experience of conquest often lurks in the background. For a community of people with collective memory of conquest in their ancestry to see a representation of their culture obliterated is, she commented, to re-experience trauma. The conversation confirmed the importance of cross-cultural leadership for multicultural work.

Meanwhile, my list of recommended contacts and participants was expanding. I found people to be responsive and interested in taking part if they could. At the end of the first week, however, I noted the one person who had not returned my phone calls or emails: Mauricio Vela. It was not hard to intuit that he was expressing an opinion about the wisdom of mediating by his silence. But I still felt it would be important to make his position explicit—and also, I valued his view of the matter and wanted it in the mix. Wondering how to make a connection, I thought about how my social network might intersect his.

When I moved into my house nearly twenty years before, I had very soon formed a warm friendship with my next-door neighbor. Helen Helfer was at that time the director of the neighborhood center, and a uniquely appreciated figure in the community. Whenever I mentioned her name, it elicited warmth and praise from my neighbors. Helen had retired some years earlier and moved away, but she and I maintained our connection, meeting each other here and there across the country as one or the other of us traveled. I knew that she had hired Mauricio to work at the center, that she thought highly of him and had supported him to succeed her when she left. So I called Helen for advice. Did she have any ideas about how I might get Mauricio to respond to me? I was fine with his participating or not, whichever he felt would be his wisest course, but I needed to talk with him either way. In the course of mobilizing a significant portion of the community, primarily people of Latino and Filipino heritage, Mauricio had stepped on a lot of toes, both in Bernal and in the city. His leadership was crucial both to the controversy and to its intensity.

"That's Mauricio!" Helen replied affectionately. She had no good advice about how to proceed, but she did say, "Give him my regards."

And so I called one more time, asking him to talk with me, whatever his views of mediation. At the end of the message I said, "My friend Helen Helfer sends her regards."

Right away, I got a call back. "Why didn't you say you're a friend of Helen's!" he exclaimed. "Any friend of Helen's has got to be good folk. Of course I'll talk with you."

This transaction was significant on several levels. It reflected the advantages of my living in community with the people I was about to mediate. The network of connections located me as a trustworthy person—at least, trustworthy enough for a conversation. That Mauricio was open to dialogue once he knew a way to link with me was also, I believed, culturally significant. The difference between relying on credentials and relying on relationships in the process of legitimizing the role of an intervener is crucial. Do people operate from within a professionalized worldview or a relational one? The distinction shows up again and again at every step of the way.

On a rainy January afternoon, Mauricio arrived at my home. We sat in my living room sharing "Helen stories" until at length I broached the topic of the mediation. Mauricio strongly expressed the opinion that it was not in his interest to participate. He was busy amassing support to save the mural and had no desire to compromise that clear and compelling claim; he saw mediation as a process of compromise in which he would have to "deal" by giving up something that his followers wanted.

Mauricio linked his current campaign with an earlier one. When the library bond had first passed, the question arose of a pre-school housed in the basement of the Bernal building. That project was something very close to Mauricio's heart. Operating through San Francisco Community College, it offered a much-needed service to low-income families. Not only was the nursery school a real benefit, but social services were also available on-site to the families of students. The amalgam of a community college–funded school housed in a local library and extending much-needed services to an underserved portion of the community, made the project very dear to Mauricio and many other lower income people in the neighborhood. Mauricio had launched a campaign to preserve the right of the school to library space, and he had lost. When the building closed for renovation, the school was permanently moved to a public school building nearby.

Mauricio still resented that outcome, and it added intensity to his current fight to save the mural on the building's exterior. At the same time, the first campaign had left scars for other people, as well, and those wounds fueled a layer of ill-feeling about this dispute. Mauricio told me his story of both issues. He very clearly stated that his larger interest was to empower the community of color on the hill, as he anticipated future potential harms deriving from continuing gentrification. To interrupt the mobilization work that was underway in order to mediate seemed to him to be contraindicated.

## When to Resolve Conflict and When to Foment It?

I could see his point. It is easy as a conflict intervener to become passionate about the work, believing that collaborative processes are innately superior to adversarial ones. There is a kind of moral positioning to which we who do this work are subject. But approaches that rely on equality of decision-making rights also assume equality of power to make those decisions. In the real world, the latter assumption is often untrue; to overlook that reality risks disadvantaging those who are already disadvantaged.

Mauricio's view of what was happening in the community rested squarely on perceptions of inequality. He believed that the interests of Latino and Filipino residents were in jeopardy of being overruled in favor of the wishes of more affluent, majority white, newer-comers to the neighborhood. The earlier experience with the pre-school reinforced that view, which also nested in a lifetime of lived incidents of discrimination and disrespect. Therefore, he saw his task as amassing power to negotiate a successful outcome to this controversy through community organizing. He got busy mobilizing his network of friends and allies. When commission hearings and other public forums took place, Mauricio brought as many advocates of Save the Bernal Library Mural as he could, and they loudly proclaimed their views, sometimes using declamatory language. In particular, Mauricio accused those who opposed him of racism, a troubled charge that ensures escalation of conflict.

Escalation was very much what any good community organizer would seek. To negotiate from a position of weakness is to lose the fight. But the means for strengthening a disenfranchised group's position are limited. By whatever means, they involve building power through coercive acts, more or less violent or nonviolent, but encompassing some form of threat. Large numbers of people standing silent vigil can make a powerful statement, as well as constitute a moral challenge. Adding vivid artwork, or slogans, or chanting, or marching, increases the effectiveness. Political theater can be creative, more or less vituperative, but it always relies upon some sort of disruptive public presence. Experienced organizer that he was, Mauricio understood these dynamics well. Based on his experiences, he did not believe that reasoned argument before the library commission was his constituents' strong suit. Many of them were working class, less educated than the opposition, less confident about public speaking. English was not the first language for some. Alternatively, then, storming meetings and sloganeering gave them a louder voice and, he hoped, a better hearing. In the heat of his own feelings, Mauricio further heightened the threat level by including in his impassioned rhetoric charges of racism.

That charge was especially onerous to the city librarian, Luis Herrera. Of Latino heritage himself, he had just been hired in 2002 when the fight over the pre-school exploded. At a reception welcoming him to San Francisco, protestors picketed noisily, and the librarian was both alarmed and offended. Now, history was repeating itself. Ardently, he wished to find a solution to the debate that calmed the community.

Meanwhile, another group of Bernal residents had organized a counterweight. They formed an ad hoc group called New Deal for Bernal, their chosen name referencing their strong advocacy for the WPA building. They, too, attended commission meetings arguing that the walls of the library be restored to their original color and look. Many of the people comprising this group enjoyed influence in the city by virtue of their positions. They knew how to keep track of commission meeting schedules, how to sign up to speak, how to present their arguments. They also all appeared to be white.

In this polarized atmosphere, Mauricio's forces were growing. Why should he turn to a negotiation that could interfere with his organizing momentum and perhaps require compromises unacceptable to the people he was championing? I had recently joined with two colleagues to write a paper addressing just this question, and I didn't agree that mediating need interfere with organizing (Burdick, Kriesberg, and Roy 2010). In fact, I could see ways they could work well together. I pointed out to Mauricio that I viewed this particular process as mediating relationships rather than resolving issues. Over the last few decades, as the population of the hill had changed, people's understanding of neighbors' diverse perspectives had lapsed, and what had once been an effectively unified community was now rent. The present dispute testified to a longer and more dire conflict. My own objective, I confessed, was to raise consciousness on all sides. And because of my work on the cusp of social divides based in identity differences, I was especially considering mediation to be an opportunity for more advantaged people to gain a greater understanding of realities of life for neighbors of color. While I fully anticipated that understanding—and I hoped sympathy—would increase in all directions, I knew that disadvantaged people often had more insight into the experiences of people on the other side of the divide than the other way around. How power is distributed in societies can generally be described in terms of a cultural bulls-eye: there are people in the center, and others more or less residing on the outer circles of the design. The center defines normalcy. Although many changes occurred in the latter half of the twentieth century, our diagram would still reflect white men in the center, with white women in the next circle out. Of course, each of those categories could—and should—be further broken down by class, religion, sexual orientation, physical ability, age, immigration status, and so on. Stratification is minute and endless; a very, very small number of people actually enjoy the privilege of residing in the exact center of the bulls-eye. But proximity to the center denotes cultural assumptions; you are more or less acculturated to certain worldviews and attitudes based on how far toward the edges of the bulls-eye your identity group is consigned. There are many ways of talking about these dynamics, none of them entirely adequate. One lens is privilege, and that is a useful lens in that it so quickly becomes apparent that privilege is a shifting and situational matter. I am privileged as a white women with a PhD, less privileged because my degree is in sociology and not biochemistry, less privileged still because I am old.

When all these factors and lenses and experiences filter down, there is very often the discrepancy I'm describing here: a young person of color living in Bernal is likely to know more about the lives of affluent white neighbors than the other way around. For me, any conflict intervention is an opportunity to extend consciousness of others' realities in all needed directions.

Mauricio was interested in this perspective. I went on to say that I thought the rhetoric he had been using had closed down the space for constructing such understandings. When people feel hurt, they stop listening—a form of self-protection that is understandable and close to universal. Argument grows and awareness diminishes. If I am ardently engaged in defending my position, I am not hearing the meanings you attach to yours. Healing some of the hurt, therefore, increases the room for more compassionate and collective solutions to the problem. His rhetorical strategy might expand numbers of supporters but cut off potentially helpful alliances and diminish chances for a negotiated success.

"Well," Mauricio said, "I suppose I could try taking part. I know I'll have to take a lot of heat. I can take the abuse, I guess."

Some heat, I acknowledged, would no doubt be involved, but no abuse. On a personal level, Mauricio seemed to me to be worn down. His manner was more exhausted than angry. I've seen these symptoms often before: people engaged in extended battle internalize injuries that they have little way of calculating, nor therefore of healing. I commented on my perception to Mauricio, and he agreed that he was indeed weary of being in the eye of the storm. "It's very hard," he said plaintively, "to have so many people angry at me." That he had not grown a skin thick enough to ward off his opponents' anger spoke well of his connection with his own heart. To me, it suggested the other side of his passion about the issue and about representing his followers. All of it spoke at least as much of vulnerability as of rage.

"Here's another reason for you to take part and heal some injuries," I said. "You'll burn out if you don't. You're far too passionate an advocate for the community to lose you that way." I then made two commitments to him:

First, during mediation no one would be mean to him—nor would I permit him to be mean to anyone else.

Secondly, I would not under any circumstances ask him—or anyone else—to compromise anything of genuine importance. Too much compromise leads to later regret, and from there to resentment and renewed conflict. If solutions were to be found, they would have to sit genuinely well with everyone involved.

On that basis, Mauricio agreed to take part.

## Composing the Group

The mediation group was taking shape. So far, in addition to Mauricio it comprised:

- Johanna Silva Waki, a Latina woman, having several generations on the hill, representing the board of the Bernal Heights Neighborhood Center as its chair;
- Larry Cruz, a gay Latino homeowner and member of that board, but taking part as an individual;
- Darcy Lee, a white woman, store owner on Cortland Avenue, and president of the Bernal Business Alliance;
- Terry Milne, a white man, longtime resident on the hill, an artist, author, and historian; and
- Susan Kelk Cervantes, a Caucasian woman, founding director of Precita Eyes Muralists, a long-established Bernal Heights nonprofit dedicated to community mural art around the Bay Area and beyond.

I continued talking with many people on both sides of the issue, including all members of the New Deal group. Although they spoke in public with a unified voice, I began to hear variation in their positions. Some objected to the mural on architectural grounds, others on aesthetic grounds. Some wanted the WPA history to be honored; others were interested in new public artwork somewhere connected with the building. Some people were very hurt and angry about Mauricio's manner in the public meetings, as well as other interpersonal experiences with him and his followers. Others were more sympathetic to the Save the Bernal Library Mural campaign even though they disagreed with it. I puzzled over how to choose the most constructive participants. In consultation with Larry, Cynthia, and other colleagues, I began to sketch criteria.

In every conversation, I asked whether the individual wanted to take part (all but two did), whether they were available to take part on the date we'd set (several were not), and if they did not take part, who in their circle of dialogue would most influence their own views as the representative's views shifted. This last question helped to map networks of leadership, the ability of certain individuals to be opinion shapers. As the conversations proliferated, certain names re-occurred, leading me in their direction.

In addition to a demographic range of ethnicities, races, ages, and genders, I clearly wanted a balance of positions, pro and con the mural. But I also assumed there was a silent majority of people who had feelings about the issue but had not spoken out in meetings. They were harder to find; no rosters existed of the ones who hadn't attended. I began asking everyone I met what they thought about the issue, as well as asking the outspoken people to identify others who either agreed or disagreed with them. I had a fair idea of what circles of people lived on the hill. There were young parents new to the community, as well as their nannies, who spent a lot of time at the playground behind the library. There were politically involved veterans of all identities—white, Latino, Filipino—who had not spoken out on the current dispute, but who I was sure would have interesting things to say about it. There were young single people who had grown up on the hill along with their parents and grandparents.

Eventually, I invited another five people:

▪ Amy Trachtenberg, a white woman mentioned often by others as respected and influential; a visual artist who had recently completed an elaborate library project in a nearby city; she expressed a wish that the Bernal mural not be restored, and was open to creative alternatives;

▪ Brandon Powell, a relative newcomer and the African-American father of young children in an interracial family; he favored preserving what could be saved of the mural;

▪ Michael Smith, also a young African-American father and a member of one of the design review committees on the hill; he identified himself as a historic preservationist and could also "see the other side";

▪ Monique Jaquez, a young Latina, third generation on the hill, an artist employed at Darcy's store; she was concerned that changing demographics of the community be reflected in the artwork; and

▪ Dan Martinez, a Latino printer, young father, active parishioner in a Catholic church on Cortland Avenue; he was a member of the Save the Bernal Library Mural committee and was proposed by Mauricio.

This group of eleven were primed and ready to meet on January 23. Although the building was not scheduled to open for another week, the library staff arranged for us to use the brand new community meeting room.

## Designing the Process

My framework for mediating was created in the early 1970s by a group called Radical Therapy. It began as a self-help technique for working through conflicts within the group, which was striving to operate collectively using consensus decision-making. Members of the collective recognized that a wish for equality was not the same as the reality. When conflicts arose, they saw them as moments of potential learning about how power worked among them and how to bring about change in the direction of equality. Believing that they needed a way to work through conflicts with respect and realistic attention to truth, they created a structure for mediation that has well stood the test of time. It parallels approaches that are widely used in community mediation and other settings, although with some important differences:

- *Homework*: Guidelines are presented to all participants for preparing. People are urged to bring with them to the session their own notes about goals, feelings, and ideal outcomes.
- *Goals*: Statements by each participant of what they would ideally like the session to accomplish.
- *Exchange of Feelings*: A structured emotional dialogue. Taking turns, participants clear the air of "held feelings" and sort out assumptions and intuitions.
- *Analysis*: The mediator presents feedback about the central dynamics of conflict. Often this analysis outlines power dynamics on both material and interpersonal planes. (This part of the process is not common to most other approaches to mediation.)
- *Negotiation*: Starting with the ideal outcome, participants recognize areas of agreement and disagreement and seek solutions where needed.
- *Plan*: Once an agreement has been reached, participants make a concrete plan for who will do what to implement it.
- *"Strokes"*: If appropriate, the session ends with an exchange of positive feelings.

I've used this template over the years and taught it to apprentices and university students. When Cynthia and I discussed the design of the Bernal work, however, this familiar structure was not foremost in my mind. In truth, I didn't know how we should proceed, so we began with the obvious: tempers were hot and relationships rent—we needed to start there. Cynthia and I both knew from long experience that putting the dispute in an analytic context would help people step away from hard feelings once their grievances had been aired, but we already had enough information to sense the need to frame the work from the beginning in a larger context, to encourage people to believe that speaking emotional truth would lead to objective changes. Whether we would ever get to a stage of negotiation was questionable. We did not want to presume that would happen lest it focus our energies too specifically on mission impossible. So we designed a process that would evolve from what we discovered in the room. Interestingly, looking back afterward, I can see how it in fact followed the main course of the steps outlined above, but with variations necessitated by the specifics of this community and this conflict. In reality, that kind of flexibility is needed in all facilitations.

Finally, Cynthia and I constructed some "homework," a series of questions for people to consider. It consisted of four parts:

1. Goals for the mediation

2. Emotional wounds (with guidelines for respectful ways to speak about them)

3. Resolution, both the ideal outcome and also a set of acceptable outcomes

4. Appreciation

The full document appears in Appendix A.

As part of my practice, I train people through an apprenticeship program. There was keen interest within that group to assist in this particular mediation. I chose Ellen Morrison, an advanced trainee who also happens to be a San Francisco muralist. I valued her knowledge of that world and her skilled insight into the identity and organizational questions embedded in the controversy.

All that remained was to arrange for creature comforts: tea and coffee, pizza for lunch, some sweet things for snacking, and the good will of the authorities. The neighborhood center volunteered for the first of these elements, and the last was eagerly extended by the various political leaders, directors, and commissioners who had been dealing with the controversy for so many years.

# 3

# The Beginning

*Goals, Roles, and Power Relations*

ON THE MORNING of January 23, 2010, we gathered in the brand-new community meeting room at the library. A long table had been set up for us. Larry brought over some flip charts and easels from the neighborhood center across the street. Another table was filled with breakfast foods, coffee, and tea. Some of the arriving participants greeted acquaintances; several knew no one in the room and introduced themselves. There was generally an air of curious anticipation and, I would say, nerves.

A man from the city library staff had opened the building for us and now led us on a tour of the building. Since I had seen it three weeks earlier, much had been accomplished. People "ooh'ed and ah'ed" in admiration for the refinished tables, the new row of computer terminals in the main reading room, the shelves filled with Spanish-language books, the teen section and children's library. The ceiling had been stenciled and signs to the various sections gilded by a brilliant young craftsman from the neighborhood. He and his wife had been hired late in the renovation process to add artistic touches that so perfectly completed the detailed reconstruction of the interior that it was hard to imagine the building without them. Our guide pointed out the gorgeous hanging light fixtures, explaining that only a few had been left intact before the renovation, but a glass-maker had been found who reproduced the art deco pieces with stunning exactitude. The library was altogether a work of art.

As we walked, I counted heads; I expected twelve people in addition to my team, including Supervisor Campos and eleven "mediatees." One person was missing: Mauricio. The mediation had begun, I thought. I fully expected Mauricio to come; I knew him to be true to his word and he'd promised to take part. But I also knew he was conflicted in that decision, so I questioned whether the hour of his arrival held meaning.

Back at the meeting room, people filled coffee cups and settled into places around the table. Through the door came Mauricio, accompanied by a young man. He introduced Giulio Sorro. Giulio was someone I had pursued to take part in the mediation but had not reached. His parents were well-known activists in the community. His dad, a beloved community organizer in the city, had died a few years earlier, mourned widely. Of Italian and Filipino heritage, Giulio taught high school history and worked with youth in the Bernal community as well. I had thought he would bring a rich perspective to the work, but his mother, whom I knew slightly and had reached by phone, had her doubts he would consent. He was out of town, she had told me, and super-busy. But she would ask; I never heard from him.

Mauricio and I had engaged in some negotiation before he had agreed to come. In his reluctance, he had suggested that he needed to begin ceding leadership to others in his group. He had been ill and he was tired. He had a desire to mentor new leadership among the young. Much as I appreciated that idea, I had argued that he had generated a good deal of controversy by his strategy and style, and there was some repair work that compelled his presence. "Well, I'll choose a couple of people and bring them along," he declared.

"No," I countered, "I'm choosing the participants. I'm happy for you to suggest some people; I'll speak with them and do my best to include them."

### Establishing the Power Landscape

It is not uncommon for negotiation of power to begin well before a mediation formally begins. This exchange with Mauricio was a key moment. I aimed to establish that I welcomed him as an ally in the work at hand, but also that I was in charge. For the work to succeed, I needed to be authorized by every participant to exercise the skills needed to manage the process constructively. I wasn't asking to dominate for the sake of my ego or position, but I was making a pragmatic intervention. I was signaling that the participants, in this case Mauricio, must accept my power to shape the process, to intervene, and, if needed, to stand up to acts of coercion. Both Mauricio and I knew that many of the choices he had made in conducting his campaign to save the mural had been just that: acts motivated by the intention to overpower his opponents and force the city authorities to decide in his favor. In this moment of paradoxical transaction, I was telling Mauricio that the mediation would proceed by different rules—collaborative, rather than adversarial—and that those rules would be facilitated by my (at the moment) dictatorial leadership.

With a twinkle of approval in his eye, Mauricio gave me several names.

Much has been written about how power works among parties in conflict, much less about the power of conflict interveners. Mediators often imagine themselves to have, or to need, little power. Keepers of process only, the role is prescribed to be neutral. A good mediator is thought to have no influence over the content of a dispute, but simply to create an environment in which parties can move from adversarial processes to collaborative ones.

Skillful mediators do often appear to be more foundation-layers than skyscraper builders. Methods like that taught by Robert Bush and Joe Folger in *The Promise of Mediation* (1994) coach leadership with a light hand. The mediator is to structure a conversation and then let participants find their own way to completion. For Bush and Folger, it is the process of dialogue rather than the outcome of settlement that empowers people to transform relations and, consequently, their view of their own capabilities.

Other mediators, more intent on settlement of the dispute at hand, may take a more active role, caucusing with sides, sometimes keeping parties entirely separate and acting as a go-between negotiator. When lawyers are involved, the primary parties may never speak with each other directly. Story-telling becomes a form of argument among representatives.

These two approaches represent the extremes. For me, it is not possible to separate relationship from problem-solving. If people haven't built sufficient openness to each other, then the hard work of resolving the dispute is unlikely to succeed. On the other hand, however affectionate people feel after moving beyond hurt and anger, good feelings may not survive long if the conflict still burns hot. I believe it is possible, indeed necessary, to address emotions, power dynamics, and settlement all in the same process. When I told Mauricio I would never ask him to compromise, I was not suggesting that no resolution would take place, but I was also not promising that one would. Instead, I believe enduring resolution to disputes only takes place when people find solutions that do not importantly compromise anyone's essential interests, and that universal satisfaction can only happen when people are genuinely negotiating with a view to taking equal care of their own interests and those of everyone else. I'll write a good deal more about this point when the mediation reaches the point of negotiation, but I was thinking about it from the beginning because it centrally informed my design of the process and my choice of participants.

Where "empowerment" comes in is both in the experience of free and respectful speech and in the capacity to construct solutions. Added to both those elements is also the fact of learning. I see myself very much as a teacher. My hope is to pass along to mediation participants conscious possession of tools for future use in conflicts. And beyond the tools themselves is a mind-set, an understanding of the meaning of consensus and an appreciation for the worldview within which consensus becomes possible.

When Mauricio arrived at the mediation late and accompanied by Giulio, I read his actions in terms of the negotiation of power we had begun earlier. I welcomed Giulio's presence even as I expressed surprise. I noted hackles rising. This moment was a negotiation of my leadership with every individual in the room, and I knew my reaction would launch a pattern. And so I responded warmly to Giulio, not to Mauricio, while also naming the problem:

"I'm glad you're here, Giulio. I had hoped to reach you last week but understood you were out-of-town. I'd have preferred to have agreed in advance that you were coming so everyone expected you and you had time to prepare. Nonetheless, you're very welcome now." Mauricio and Giulio took their seats.

Conflict intervention often challenges the mediator with situations that, like this one, require quick strategic decision-making. I think of these moments as subtle and fluid negotiations of leadership. Would it have been wise to respond with clear adherence to a rule: "I choose the participants! Giulio must leave." That tact would have asserted my procedural power with a no-mistake-about-it clarity. But in this moment, that was not the kind of leadership I sought. Instead, I hoped the participants would grant Cynthia and me authority to lead a process at the same time they claimed the process as their own. I wanted them to join with us and with each other, and so I quickly decided the wiser path was to join with Mauricio in his act of bringing Giulio into the group rather than to oppose him. That decision was supported by my genuine interest in having Giulio participate. I anticipated—very correctly as it turned out—that he would make important contributions.

And so we moved right along. We had arranged for Supervisor Campos to open the meeting, ritualizing his role as sponsor. He spoke very briefly, welcoming folks and stating his hopes, including the hope that he could stay and observe the work. He was fascinated by the process, he said, and wanted to learn at the same time that he supported what we were doing. But David could hardly become a fly on the wall. He was a person who exercised considerable influence in the city; as time went on, he could deploy his power in many different ways. In the end he might prove to be ally or adversary to any individual in the room or to the collective outcome. Pure observation by a person with powers lying outside the room—in this case by virtue of his political position—is not possible.

On the other hand, David also exemplified another domain in which power operates: the personal. He was an unusual politician, his manner enormously open, inviting trust. He was young and relatively new on the community landscape. I didn't know with certainty how different people in the room felt about him, but I was so far impressed with how he had conducted himself. He read to me, and I suspected to most others, as an honest man.

If he was to stay, which I thought was likely to be an advantage to the work, it was essential to craft his role with care, a conversation I now initiated. I expressed what I've written here, what I believed to be the virtues and dilemmas of his presence. On the one hand, his support for the process inspired our work and also suggested his will to advocate for resources to fund whatever conclusion we came to, should we come to a consensus. On the other hand, powers David might exercise outside the room could influence what happened inside it. His power could be used for good or ill. If anyone feared the latter, then the space to speak freely would likely be compromised.

Fear is an emotion that I respect. It is an animal response to perceived danger. In that moment when a gazelle scents a lion, it freezes, assessing the perception and, suffused with adrenaline, deciding how the wind blows and whether to bolt. Human abilities to assess the reality of danger are handicapped by the greater complexity of the dangers we face. Sometimes that complexity is layered with past experiences that inform the possibility of danger that may not actually threaten in the present moment. Most of us have some experience, firsthand or through the media, of double-dealing politicians. Yet here sat David, a warm and seemingly trustworthy man, a person carrying a human heart as well as the mantle of his office. In the context of mediation, fear is a manifestation of power dynamics. If I fear I am not safe to speak, then my power in the mediation, a process almost entirely dependent on speech, is severely compromised.

I might have asked the participants to say whether they feared consequences to his presence. But the contradiction in doing that is this: if people lack power to protect themselves from some potential harm, they may also lack the safety to speak that fear. So instead, I asked David to address the concern, and he was warmly reassuring. He declared his great respect for everyone in the room and his clear intention to be nothing but supportive. In other mediations,

I've asked the person in leadership to leave the room at this point, so others can speak freely about their fears and needs. In this case, again acting on instinct, I agreed that David could stay on the condition that he remain silent unless questions or comments were addressed directly to him. I polled the people around the table and believed the agreement they expressed.

There was one more piece of business for us to accomplish before we began the content of the mediation. As with mediator neutrality, confidentiality is another feature of conflict intervention that is deeply assumed in a culture to which professionalism and individualism are central. Deriving from both legal and therapeutic roots of conflict resolution, confidentiality is intended to protect parties from harmful consequences were information to be extended beyond the control of those present. When participants vow not to speak of what goes on inside the room outside the room, we imagine that we've constructed a safe space in which to speak.

All that makes sense; we do live in a world that can be litigious and judgmental. However, there's a practical matter of possibility. It is only human that people going through new and intense experiences want and need to talk about them. Consulting with others can provide support, a place to sound off without the discipline required in the course of structured discourse, a source of input from a different perspective or of nurturing to help heal something painful that has happened. "Pillow talk" is legion; at the end of the day, we want to share what we've been through with intimate others.

In every mediation, therefore, I explore in some detail what confidentiality really means. Sometimes there is a need to specify "safe" sources of support. Often it is helpful to acknowledge that people will talk outside the room and therefore to construct an agreement about *how* they'll talk: with care for the well-being of others, without judgment or an intention to spread ill feeling.

In a community mediation, the matter is even more complex. I knew that many of the people in the room were viewed as representatives by people not in the room. They were sure to be asked by their "constituents" what had happened, and those fellow community members had a right to know. At the same time, the goodwill we hoped and intended to restore through our process was a delicate matter, at least in the beginning; hopefully it would grow sturdy and robust as time went on. So we vowed to talk at the end of the day in some detail about what and how our proceedings should be reported out.

# 4

# Storytelling

## *Emotion and Meaning*

NOW WE WERE READY to begin in earnest. We asked people to introduce themselves and say what their primary reasons were for taking part. What were the goals they hoped the mediation would achieve? Answers fell into three categories: to heal emotional wounds, to understand better the history and meanings involved, and to resolve the question in order to move on to a "bright new look" for the library. Occasionally, goals people bring to mediation are mutually exclusive; these were compatible, even though we knew that goals for the ultimate fate of the library were widely divergent. As a mediator, I listen to the goal-setting part of the process for my instructions: What specifically am I assigned to mediate? That question gives rise, of course, to the next question: Can I in fact do what is being asked? There is a distinction, often hard for people to make, between *goals for an intervention* and *hopes for particular outcomes* to the conflict. Insofar as our framework embraced the objective to change understandings and relationships, each of the goals articulated was compatible with the others. A "bright new look," however, was a different matter. Although I continued to hold to my original offer to mediate community relations but not necessarily the library artwork, I pointed out that emotional healing and deeper understanding might bring about a climate in which new ideas could emerge. Heated conflict tends to narrow imagination, cementing ideas in solidified positions. I didn't rule out the possibility that a different and more respectful kind of dialogue might produce a new framework in which to resolve the issue itself.

Sometimes, disagreement in a more compassionate relational environment gives rise to a more abundant set of possibilities to negotiate.

Cynthia and I acknowledged the goals and framed the discussion we were about to have. Based on the public record and my many interviews with community members, we noted the interlocking levels involved. The mural on the library was the current dispute, surrounded by ongoing dynamics in the neighborhood. Gentrification had brought with it interpersonal and cultural changes, and the economics of change had displaced people with strong links to the community. Those changes were in turn seated in national dynamics involving class, race, and ethnicity, and global dynamics of economic development. We felt it was important to note the various elements interwoven with the current controversy in order to signal our willingness for people to talk about it all. Nothing was to be ruled out of the discourse.

But the work was best begun in the room, we suggested, on the human level of emotional damage. We invited people to first clear the air of anything they were feeling that might get in the way of a genuinely cooperative spirit. We presented some guidelines for speaking both honestly and respectfully. The tool we used is a variation on the common form of "I statements," a form called variously "held feelings," "resentments," "action-feeling statements," and "stamps." I like that last jargon; it refers to the old days when S&H Green Stamps were given to consumers in return for purchases at gas stations and grocery stores. You took them home and pasted them in a little book. When your book was full, you took it to a depot and traded it in for toasters and irons and other goodies. In the case of hard feelings, we often don't speak them for fear of hurting someone's feelings or getting into a fight. Or perhaps we see them as petty, believing it is morally superior to set them aside and hope they'll go away. But they don't; instead, they get pasted in an emotional book and, when it's full, traded in for an uproar.

The basic form we suggested is a two-part sentence: "When you did/said/didn't do [describe an action], I felt [name emotions]." The premise behind the statement is that feelings are not right or wrong, they simply are. Unexpressed, they fester. Once spoken, however, two things happen: there is some relief for the speaker from the tension that goes along with silence. And the hearer, who is instructed truly to listen and not to respond right away, learns something of the speaker's internal world. Later, both people can decide whether the emotional information requires a discussion. Sometimes, speaking is sufficient. Other times, active attention is needed. But the emotional din that so often is produced by hearing that you've somehow harmed another person—the impulse to argue, defend, apologize, collapse into guilt— interferes with meaningful dialogue. So waiting is wise.

We finished our teaching . . . and the group sat thoughtfully, per- haps nervously, silent for a few beats. Then Brandon asked, "What do you mean by gentrification? Why use that term?"

Giulio responded, giving us a fascinating history of San Francisco and of Bernal Heights. He talked about growing up in the neighbor- hood and the changes he had personally experienced. He told stories of new people moving in and scolding teenagers for playing ball in the street, something the kids had always done. "The problem for me is not change," he concluded. "It's entitlement. I see it as part of white privilege, and I resent it."

Mauricio next commented on the economic impact of escalating home prices, especially the consequences to the business district of the community. Prices in stores rose so that people who had always shopped on Cortland Avenue now went to less affluent streets. "We shop on Mission Street now," he said, referencing the heavily Latino district abutting Bernal.

Darcy quickly countered. She was fairly bouncing in her seat with agitation. She addressed a Held Feeling to Mauricio: "When you said you only shopped on Mission St., I felt hurt." She went on to say that she thought he believed the neighborhood changes were altogether bad, that the merchants on Cortland made no contributions to the community. This statement is a good example of a very familiar phe- nomenon. Darcy had heard words Mauricio spoke and reacted emo- tionally. At the same time, she read between the lines, imagining a larger meaning that was personally injurious to her. In provocative opposition to psychiatric theory, the radical therapy orientation out of which we work calls this process of creating interpretative stories *paranoia*. We reclaim the word "paranoia" from psychiatry, insisting that people are not crazy or projecting. Instead, we try to account for things we pick up but which are not overtly expressed. *Paranoia*, we contend, is heightened awareness. Our intuitions, interpretations, fears—the process can take many forms—are always based in some kernel of truth. However, if denied or kept secret, that kernel can grow into a distorted story. We then become wedded to the explanations we've constructed, believing them to be true. The more they are denied, the more we cling to them.[1]

One of the most respectful acts of communication is to speak the kernel of truth. After it has been acknowledged, correcting whatever distortions have crept in is easy. Once we know what is true, we're far more likely to be willing to hear what is not true.

In this case, Cynthia urged Mauricio to tell Darcy what she had correctly intuited. He said he had been hurt by gentrification twice in his lifetime. The nearby neighborhood where he had grown up had become so costly that he had been forced to move to Bernal, which now was going the same way. Twice he had seen his community torn apart by the same economic dynamics. He spoke of his personal sense of failure as well. "I've always tried to create level playing fields," he said, "and that's not happened." On the other hand, he also acknowledged that Darcy and other merchants had personally made contributions to the community. Cortland was now a safer street; the merchants sponsored community activities such as a rousing Halloween night of trick or treating, unchallenged by traffic.

The spirit in the room grew a mite more relaxed. Several people around the table leaned forward, inspired by this exchange to a readiness to speak. Dan told Darcy how hurt and angry he'd been when she

---

1. In the present volume, *paranoia* is italicized when referencing the radical therapy view and usage of this term to distinguish it from common or clinical usage. For a more detailed discussion, see chap. 12, n.1.

had posted a petition in her store calling for the removal of the mural and demeaning the quality of the art. Amy addressed Mauricio; at a meeting he had referred to his opponents as "white racist gentrifiers." She felt shocked and really sad. Susan followed with a Held Feeling for Mauricio as well: when he called the artwork on the library a "Latino mural," she felt bothered because she found it polarizing. We pointed out that "polarizing" was an idea, not a feeling, and asked her what she felt when she thought Mauricio was polarizing the controversy; she thought for a moment and said, "Hurt."

Until Susan had spoken, each of the exchanges had been "cross camp." Darcy and Mauricio had been leaders of opposite sides, and Amy and Dan had also been strongly identified with different positions. But Susan was seen as a close ally of Mauricio's. When she cleared up a complaint with her ally, she opened the territory for more dimensional dialogue.

From the first, Brandon had interjected thoughts and questions. He was bold and courageous, intent on naming elephants and insisting on honesty. Now he spoke reflectively, but with an edge of emotion in his voice: "Here's what I want to know," he said. "How long do you have to live in this neighborhood before you have standing?"

The expression of feelings went on for some time longer. Again and again, we returned to two words: entitlement and standing. To frame the dispute in these terms was to open grounds for discussion on the basis of understandable and respect-worthy human wishes. *Entitlement* suggested that everyone in the community had equal rights to well-being and respect. *Standing* connoted a desire to belong, to have one's needs respected. And so the two emotionally-potent expressions converged at a very human point.

At length, the moment seemed right to shift the discourse to a different form. We proposed that everyone state their position about the mural, while Ellen, my apprentice, mapped their statements on a long piece of paper spanning one wall. As each person spoke, a dimensional picture emerged of a range of sentiments. Even those who agreed that the mural should stay or the mural should go expressed different reasons. More ideas were added to the mix: a new mural should be painted by the community; new artwork should be created, but not a mural; the side and back walls should be painted but the Cortland façade left bare.

We broke for lunch, an opportunity for people to mix companionably. The tension of the morning seemed lessened. There was laughter, small-talk, appreciation.

## Elaborating Positions

After lunch, however, we ramped up the process. Ellen had drawn a vivid map of the range and subtleties of positions. We now directed people to caucus, to gather in whatever groupings of shared thinking they wanted, and to craft clear and thorough statements of the arguments for their position. The relaxation of lunchtime was gone in a flash. Three people seated themselves at the "no mural" end of the table: Darcy, Amy, Terry—three Anglo people. At the other end, all but two of the remaining group clustered around Susan, who set about explaining the images on the original mural. In the middle of the table, Monique and Michael, both young, one Latina, the other African-American, sat side by side talking animatedly.

Observing from the sidelines, Cynthia and I noted that the "no mural" grouping was unhappy. The numbers were against them. In our democratic majority-centric culture, numbers count. I wandered over to them and listened as they ran out their fears. Susan was delivering a lecture, they declared; people were being swayed by her narrative. It was not fair. I reassured them that it was all part of a work-in-progress. I urged them to stay focused on the task we had given them. Write down all their most compelling reasons for wanting clean walls. I knew they could uphold their position admirably.

We spent easily an hour on the process. At the end of the allotted time, we asked one spokesperson from each group to report out the results. Whatever their size, each group was ensured equal voice. Cynthia urged people to listen with their most open ears. "Imagine walking in the other person's shoes," she advised. The reasons given for each position were thoughtful and, often, exactly parallel. The "no mural" group wanted to honor the building and its WPA architect.

The "restored mural" group wanted to honor Arch Williams, the original muralist, and the community members who found particular images meaningful. The "in between" group wanted to honor the community by making the images reflect the current population of the hill. On the one side, people argued that the mural reflected community ownership. On the other, that the mural did not reflect the uses of the building.

It was proving difficult for people to listen without arguing. We intervened to reassure them that the time would come for discussion. Right now, we were hearing what people wanted and the brief version of why. Later, we would spell out stories that fleshed out the "why," building a better basis for understanding and therefore for discussion. At the moment, our task was simply to record the statements on Ellen's chart, to map the territory without exploring it. When all groups had spoken fully, we regarded the wall. It was a portrait of dignified and reasonable wishes and beliefs. Most importantly, we regarded a continuum rather than two statements in opposition to each other. Some people who wanted to restore the mural wanted to do so to honor the initial artist, while others wanted to preserve meaningful representations of the community in the past. Some people wanted to reinterpret the mural and update it to reflect changes in the community in the present, while others wanted to produce entirely new artwork. Some people wanted the exterior to revert to a style and color that was historically accurate, while others wanted no mural but new colors. What had been eclipsed by the hot light of argument before uninvolved decision-makers (the commissioners), in a calmer environment emerged as dimensional and varied.

So what should we do next? Our scheduled five hours were fast approaching conclusion. Without hesitation, people wanted to meet again—and soon. I knew Cynthia would not be able to come. I hoped Ellen would, and I was ready to do whatever was needed. It is always somewhat miraculous to find a time when fifteen busy people can get together, but the group had little difficulty deciding on Tuesday evening, two days hence. Larry offered his living room. And Supervisor

Campos asked permission to continue to sit in, easily and unanimously granted.

I read the willingness of the group to continue on as both dedication to the work we had begun, and engagement in what we had so far done. We exchanged some acknowledgements and left the library, tired and inspired.

## A Power Scan

Throughout the mediation process, power is a concept in the forefront of my consciousness. It is enormously useful as a way of understanding relationships among people in multiple contexts at a given moment. Some time ago, during a conversation about how power was working in a given example, Cynthia asked whether there might be a way to create a tool for performing a "power scan." I thought that a splendid idea. I can't say we've built a tool exactly, but I have written up the way in which I think power is at work in daily life.

Juliana Birkhoff conducted a study some years back, looking at how conflict resolvers conceptualize power (Birkhoff 2000). Most, she found, think of power as "a thing," a resource that people either possess or lack. Lawyers tended to define power in terms of negotiation positions: people either possess "BATNA"—"best alternative to a negotiated agreement"—and therefore advantage in negotiation, or "WATNA"—"worst alternative to a negotiated agreement."

Juliana argued that power is in reality not a resource or a measure of relative strength in negotiation, but rather a process. It is a way that we behave in relationship to other people. Following her lead, I theorize power as a process happening in several domains simultaneously:

> • Internal: How do you feel and think about your own capabilities? This dynamic can, of course, be highly situational: I feel very much more capable when I'm the professor in front of a class than when I'm in front of a judge pleading my case for forgiving a traffic ticket. When in our first meeting Mauricio talked about his battle weariness and his desire to cultivate new leadership so that he could

step back, he was expressing something he was experiencing on an emotional level that impacted his willingness to mediate. It was a somewhat paradoxical assessment of his power: on the one hand, he recognized how much power he wielded as a leader and organizer of his community, and on the other hand he sensed his waning energy to carry on. We all carry in our consciousness similar assessments, sometimes based on the realities of our situation, sometimes influenced by stories we carry that undermine our sense of our own capabilities. Out of that mixture, we sometimes take action, sometimes remain passive.

▪ Interactional: How do the actions of people communicate power? Whether intentionally or not, we act within a framework of power dynamics all the time. When Mauricio arrived late for the mediation session and accompanied by Giulio, some people no doubt interpreted his actions as power plays, acts intended to demonstrate his determination to exercise his will, perhaps even to impose his will on others. Mauricio's actual intentions may well have been self-protective (at a later time, he agreed that his lateness was intentional but explained the reasons in emotional rather than strategic terms; we'll come to that interaction in time). But there is a difference between intention and impact. Whatever may motivate us to act in particular ways, the impact on others may be quite different from what we intend. In either case, the interaction conveys meanings that engage negotiations of power. How loudly people talk, how entitled they feel to speak, how sure they are of being heard, all contribute to shaping the power of an individual in interaction with others.

▪ Organizational: Almost all human interaction takes place in the context of some form of institutional life. In the library the morning of the mediation, Cynthia and I were exercising power by virtue of our institutional role. We were the authorized leaders of the process, and we used that power to structure the composition and plan of the meeting. In addition, we interacted with participants in ways I've described to construct explicit and implicit agreements that granted us powers to interrupt, teach, advocate, and perform all the other roles that constitute good mediating. Our organizational power manifested as interactional power. Some of the participants also expressed organizational power, appearing in the discourse both as individuals and as representatives of more or less legitimate organizations. Johanna spoke for the Neighborhood Center, a long-established, well-legitimized, legally structured community institution. Mauricio frequently invoked his role as spokesperson for the Save the Bernal Library Mural organization, an ad hoc group whose legitimacy was contested by others. So also was the authority of the New Deal for Bernal, the other group formed specifically to contest the particular issue at hand. Interestingly, while Darcy and perhaps Amy had elements of agreement and association with that group, and Darcy certainly felt a responsibility to reflect their group, neither formally invoked the group during the mediation. Occasionally, Darcy did speak for the more recognized institution she led, the Bernal Business Alliance. Organizational power resides in the domain of named institutions, and it also plays on a field of less defined but nonetheless influential organizations: the Bernal community, the community of young parents, the Latino community, and so on. These identity groups enter into power dynamics by virtue of their meaning and their ability to mobilize resources, whether number of adherents or money or the many other forms of resource that matter in a particular moment of time.

▪ Cultural: Culture is something everyone knows to be real yet is experienced and defined in a multiplicity of ways. It is a system of shared meanings, a set of rituals, particular languages and the structures of thought associated with them, and so much more. Cultural differences can theoretically be power-neutral, but in reality they rarely are. In the real world, which is to say our political world, difference becomes domination. Some cultures are normalized, others must contend for recognition. Cultures therefore become identities invoked to justify political claims. At the same time, in most multicultural discourse, there are unstated assumptions underlying speech, ideas and meanings believed by those of a dominant identity to be "normal" and therefore beyond articulation. But for those who live in less politically powerful cultures, mainstream assumptions may grate; they are distinct constructs that must be deciphered and negotiated. One aspect of that process is about meaning, another about values. If my assumptions about right and wrong are inconsistent with those of the mainstream culture in which I live, I may find myself frequently unable to make myself understood and believed. Identity is intricately interlaced with culture; race, gender, ethnic origins, class, and so on all powerfully shape worldviews, assumptions, and ways of behaving. In the Bernal mural dispute, culture lay at the heart of the matter, both as a central factor in the mobilization of identity groups and in the object of dispute: a mural, a work of art framed in a particular historical culture with current political meanings.

▪ Social structural: Often the most difficult domain to see clearly, it is also often the most significant. Not accidentally, matters of culture and structure intersect. Those who do not enjoy the benefits of membership in the dominant culture also characteristically suffer greater exclusion from access to resources. As I write this paragraph, an email has arrived in my in-box with the subject, "Access to Paid Sick Days Less Common Among Workers of Color." The study cited also shows that white women are slightly less likely than white men to have paid sick days (IWPR, 3/15/11). Statistics like these suggest interlocking factors of race, gender, and class—the latter a topic rarely named in American discourse. The Bernal mural conflict was deeply imbedded in experiences of inequality rooted in social structure. Huge dynamics of economic change and organization—capitalism, globalization, the mushroom growth of digital industry, and more—impacted how children playing ball in their home streets were treated and how they experienced their world. The bond measure enabling branch library renovation was passed at a moment of burgeoning resources, but enacted in a time of financial constraint. Had there been ample funding available to create new art, might the question before us have been very different, more a matter of creativity and collaboration than of scarcity?

As you can no doubt see, none of the five domains I've delineated here is independent of the others. All intertwine in a rich fabric of human endeavor. Why does power matter? It is not, as some thinkers would say, that humans are intrinsically aggressive and selfish, but rather because we seek the means to construct the lives we wish to live.

One more word on the subject: there is a distinction between power—a good thing when exercised cooperatively with others—and *power plays*: acts intended to coerce others to do our bidding. Which was Mauricio's lateness at the very beginning of the mediation? Perhaps a bit of both: for him an act of self-value, for others an act of coercion. The larger question is whether the domain of interaction is operating within agreements to be cooperative, whether every individual involved has signed on to respect for every individual's well-being. That question agitated the next stage of the mediation and had to be answered with conviction.

# 5

# Analysis

*Getting to the Heart of the Matter*

EARLY THE NEXT MORNING, Darcy emailed me an anxious message. I called her, preferring voice to screen. Email is too flat a medium for conducting emotional conversation with any nuance. Darcy freely ran out her feelings: she felt guilty she hadn't represented people well, hadn't spoken powerfully enough about the "clean walls" position. In one week, 250 people had signed a petition in her store to remove the mural. But representation in the mediation didn't reflect that groundswell; she'd been talking with Amy and they agreed the composition of the group was seriously imbalanced. They felt outnumbered. They were also upset about Susan's role: Wasn't it a conflict of interest for her to take part in the mediation when she also headed a mural organization potentially in competition for a contract?

I said I was relieved she was calling me to express her feelings. Was part of what upset her about me, since I was the one who had determined the composition of the group? If so, I was very ready to hear her "held feelings." It would be a real problem if she simply went away feeling resentful—kudos to her for clearing her book of stamps at the first opportunity.

Here I insert a note about the human frailties of the mediator: I was relieved she had gotten in touch, and I was also tired. After working so hard, I heard criticism with some effort. In general, I try to listen for what is true and useful for me as a practitioner. I was not at all surprised that the small group of three at the "no mural" end of the table were alarmed. It often happens that grouping people in the way I had creates an apparent imbalance. Perhaps I hadn't left sufficient time for people to deal with how they experienced the numbers at the table in the moment, a thought I expressed to Darcy now.

I reminded Darcy of a formulation Cynthia had made that I found helpful. She had urged people to walk in others' shoes. I appreciated that it was difficult to do when you felt overpowered, but I didn't at all see Darcy's position that way. She had spoken eloquently about her feelings for the library building, representing the sentiments of others I had interviewed who shared her perspective. Our primary goal so far was in any case to clear the air and rebuild relationships, and in that regard she had been a leader. Insofar as we had moved on to a dialogue about the content of the dispute, I pointed out that the structure of the exercise ended up equalizing the positions of the people present: her position and that of people who wanted to keep the mural commanded equal respect on Ellen's chart. Besides, numbers were of little consequence when any decisions we made would be consensually. I made the same promise to Darcy I had made to Mauricio: I would not allow any individual's interests to be overwhelmed by any other's.

I suggested we make a date to bring Amy into the conversation, and we set up a time to talk in a couple of days.

## Aftershocks: Support between Sessions

Any mediation that takes longer than one sitting is likely to present a need for work outside the room. Between Saturday and Tuesday, several people were in touch with me. These conversations were opportunities for me to take stock of how things were going, and also to further the teaching about how to translate raw feeling into respectful communication. I also knew that other people were conferring with those who shared their positions. Amy and Darcy were clearly a "caucus" in the Bernal mediation. They shared a position, although, as it developed, for somewhat different reasons. They also shared identity features and were acquainted in their daily lives.

I was glad, therefore, that they turned to each other and subsequently to me. The day after Darcy and I talked, Amy sent me a message she had written in response to an inquiry from a prominent "no mural" advocate. After summarizing the steps of the mediation in a clear and evenhanded way, she wrote:

> It seemed clear that Darcy, Terry Milne and I were in the minority as far as those wishing for the Cortland St. mural to go—there was another core of folks that are somewhat in the middle, listening to both sides and thinking about compromises, most or all of whom have not been to any prior meetings—"leave some of the mural, update some of the mural . . . this and some of that," which doesn't to my mind achieve much . . . but we are talking in civil ways towards the real goal of healing the community, hopefully with art as a mechanism for doing so.

I wrote to Amy reiterating my willingness to talk with her and Darcy. I also offered a different perspective on minority/majority dynamics:

> I can certainly see why you both felt in a minority, and I'm happy to talk with you, too, about that. There are two things I'd like to suggest for the moment: First, there are actually 5 people who stated a position that included no mural on the Cortland side, and only 3 who clearly argued for a mural on that façade. Sometimes minority and majority positions are hard to read when majorities are switched in terms of other factors, which I think they were on Saturday.
>
> The second reassurance I want to give you is that I'm conducting a consensus process. What that means is that a minority of one has as much power as a majority of all-but-one. I'll do some teaching about consensus decision-making when we begin on Tuesday, including some very concrete how-to's for getting there.

If anyone went away from the outcome of our work feeling they had been overpowered, then the work would have failed. We seemed to be moving in the direction of negotiating a solution. Even though I still felt skeptical about our chances, I was very clear that any such decision would be made consensually, which meant that the process would continue until every point of view had been satisfied, however many or few people held it.

When we talked together shortly before the next session, I asked Amy and Darcy each to articulate their feelings, for the sake of getting my help formulating what they had to say in the session in ways that would be constructive. They worked conscientiously on doing their part, including suggesting some things we might do in the session itself, to bring to life background information about the murals and the building. When we met that evening at Larry's home, Amy led off with what might have been a contentious exchange. Instead, it turned out to set a tone for the evening that was enormously helpful.

**Setting Tones and Frameworks**

Before getting down to business on Tuesday, I suggested that people "warm up" with something called the "cultural name exercise." Its point is to offer a way for people to get acquainted that goes beyond appearances, pleasantries, and shared work. I invited people to choose a partner, ideally the person in the room they knew least well, and then to take turns telling the story of their names. There are always reasons why parents chose the names they gave their children. Those stories often are windows into the cultural frameworks of the family. My own first name came out of Louisa May Alcott. As an adult I once asked my mother why she had chosen the daughter who, in *Little Women*, died. My mother was horrified; she had remembered the names wrong and thought she had named me for Jo, the heroine of the novel. Meanwhile, my birth and present surnames speak to histories of pogroms, immigration, resettlement, and, in my adulthood, my own determination for cultural expansion.

The room buzzed with good feeling and laughter as the stories went on. When I called the group to reconvene, the sense of community was all the stronger for people having explored differences.

I introduced the evening's work with some reflections of my own. In my talks with people since Saturday, I had heard one refrain on all sides, summed up in the sentence, "We never win." It did not surprise me that, at this moment in our mediation, people would be experiencing anxiety in the form of a sense of powerlessness. Now, I wanted to ask people to rethink each part of that sentence:

- "We": Who is your "we"? People who agree about the fate of the mural? People who share your social identity? People who live on your part of Bernal hill?
- "Never": What lies behind your sense of inevitability? What past experiences inform it? What's the story in your mind about why you always lose? Why are you doomed to lose this time?
- "Win": What does losing mean? What are the stakes being contested?

I went on to talk about consensus, a process with no winners or losers. I taught a bit about the history and cultural forms of consensus-building and defined our goal as sufficiently taking care of each person's most essential interests that no one came away a loser.

Finally, I presented a model for thinking outside the box of apparent positions. I drew on a concept articulated by Maire Dugan that she calls nested conflict theory (Dugan 1996):

The immediate issue (in our case, the fate of the mural) nests in a web of relationships (for us, hard feelings built up over the years of past conflicts, and wounds from the present process, as well). These relationships exist in the context of particular social systems, both

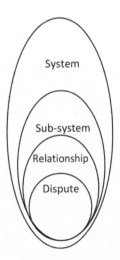

Figure 1: Nested conflict theory.

immediate (Bernal communities and cultures) and global (capitalist real estate markets, racism, class inequality, etc.).

Our mediation process might not have a measurable impact on the system level. In addition, we might not even resolve the issue. But we could impact the middle two arenas; we could make a major change in relationships among us and, in the process, impact the nature of the sub-system, the Bernal community in which we live our daily lives.

A way to start that process was to keep our relationships honest, so I invited people to begin the meeting by clearing the air. Amy raised her hand.

She asked Mauricio if she might clear up an interaction from the earlier meeting. He agreed (not without some anxiety, I thought, remembering our pre-mediation conversation). On Saturday, Mauricio had made a comment about a photographic exhibit at the library some years earlier. He pointed out critically that the people featured were all eastern European. A woman of eastern European Jewish ancestry, Amy had been silently offended. Now, she reminded him of

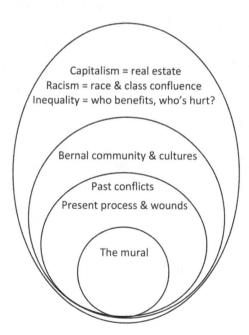

Figure 2: Nested theory applied to Bernal library mural conflict.

his remark and said it caused her to feel hurt and worried. Mauricio—
and others in the room—looked confused, so I asked Amy to formulate her *paranoia*,[1] the meaning she made of the words he spoke. "I
thought 'eastern European' was code for something anti-Semitic," she
said. Mauricio looked shocked.

"I had no idea those words might seem anti-Semitic," he declared.
"What I did mean is that they were all European, all white. I don't
know why I said 'Eastern,' but I'll think about where that came from."

We don't really know what "energy" means in the sense in which
it's commonly used in modern discourse, but whatever it is, the energy
in the room measurably shifted. Half the people present now came forward to clear up interchanges with others. Mauricio seemed relieved
when only one statement was directed to him; clearly his leadership
did not make him a target of anger in the hostile way he had feared.
Many of the exchanges brought out very moving understandings.
For example, Darcy expressed anger to Giulio about his description
of newer neighbors as feeling entitled, believing he lumped her into
that description, that he saw her as entitled. He validated that he had
feared that was true about her, but now the idea was rapidly dissipat-
ing. The more they talked, the more he saw her as dimensional. She
replied in turn that she was coming to understand his experience in
general and could see why he might have thought such a thing about
her in particular.

**From Positions to Deeper Meanings**

Facilitating emotional exchanges like these lies at the heart of the work
of mediation. Emotion is both a connecting force and a powerful way
of deepening shared contexts for understanding disparate experiences.
It is also intensely focused work for the mediator. I was, alas!, working without Cynthia's partnership from this evening forward. It is
always wonderful to co-mediate, but sometimes it just isn't possible.
I did continue to consult with her, and with Ellen, as well, between

---

1. See chap. 12, n.1 regarding the radical therapy usage of this term.

sessions. Together, we had crafted an agenda and some suggestions for people to consider before the meeting. The memo is presented in Appendix B.

After the moving interpersonal dialogue that opened the meeting, my intuition suggested it was time we plunge into the meat of the evening: going beyond positions to articulate very thoroughly the interests and meanings that lay behind them. This step is crucial for negotiating change—which we still were not committed to doing. On a relational level, however, it seemed to me to be equally important that people understand the deep roots of the positions they had been arguing so ardently. On Saturday, we had learned what each individual wanted; now we needed to know why they wanted it. I urged them each to take a turn and to speak as long as they needed in order fully to say what lay behind their desired outcomes.

Terry, our historian, began with a fascinating story of the library in the context of the community's history. Terry is a writer, illustrator, and dedicated amateur historian. He had lived on the hill for decades, actively participating in the life of the community. He was the elder of the group, soft-spoken, humorous, often merrily provocative. When he spoke now, he held everyone's attention, telling the story of the architect's national prestige and how important it had been that a person of his renown had agreed to design the building. It was one of only three significant structures in the neighborhood, he said. When it had been completed, it had signified a growing stature for the community as a whole, at a time when it was generally neglected as a working class residential area. The building itself had therefore been a potent symbol of overcoming disregard based in class.

Amy, a public artist, spoke about the history of interior murals in WPA buildings. San Francisco is known for a number of them, including a Diego Rivera mural painted for the Golden Gate International Exposition the same year the Bernal library was built; today, the mural is housed at San Francisco City College. But murals, she said, were not typical on exteriors. Amy pointed out the ways the Bernal mural conflicted with the architecture, the impermanence of weather-vulnerable artworks, and the impossibility of funding effective maintenance. She went on to sketch a number of creative ideas for alternatives, ranging from developing a plaza on the grounds to making public art elsewhere.

Giulio talked about growing up with the mural. He emphasized the impact it made when, as a child, he walked past the images of women, and especially women of color. He grew eloquent talking about the history of struggle for social justice evoked by the quotations, and the dignity the mural accorded people who all too often experience institutional alienation. Finally, he saw the mural as a symbol of unity in the community. As a project and as a product, it embodied a great range of diversity.

Next, Dan rose and unfurled large reproductions of the original mural. Dan is a printer, with a wonderfully artistic bent. He grew up in the neighborhood, and his family still lived on the hill. From old images he'd collected, he'd created the scrolls he now displayed. Everyone moved around the room, gathering on one side where we could see the images as Dan arrayed them around the floor. There were oohs and aahs, and expressions of gratitude for Dan's work. He began to tell the story of the various sections of the mural.

## The Connecting Powers of Truth and Emotion

What happened next was a pivotal event. While Dan pointed out features of the mural, Mauricio, Giulio, and others exclaimed with pleasure as they recognized images long since faded to obscurity, as if greeting old friends. They talked about the memorial to Arturo Duran, the young man who had been killed in gang violence while the mural was being created. His image on the side of the library was meant as a personal commemoration and a statement about youth violence. Someone pointed out a car on the back of the library, an old model sedan. The guys laughed and reminisced. "Look, there's the bomb. Of course, there had to be a bomb in the mural!" they chuckled fondly. Darcy was curled, relaxed, in an armchair, clearly enjoying the activity. "A lowrider?" she exclaimed. "I love lowriders!"

Dan, a moment ago laughing, turned red. Voice frozen, he said, "No, not a lowrider. A 1948 Oldsmobile. I have one in my garage right now."

The room grew very still. I could see that Dan was deciding whether to say more; emotion moved vividly across his face. "There it is," he said quietly. His voice gained intensity as he went on. "I'm a stereotype. I've always been a stereotype and I always will be, no matter what I do. I've learned a trade, made a family. I earn a good living, but I'm still a stereotype." His voice shook with feeling as the words flowed.

Darcy curled more tightly into the chair. "I'm really sorry," she said. "But I don't understand. Will you explain it to me?" Her voice was tense but warm and sad and deeply respectful. Clearly, she really did want to understand.

So Dan ran out the difference between a lowrider and a bomb, which might be any prized car. He was a collector of vintage automobiles, owned several treasured ones. Dan spoke himself into dimensionality, enthusiastic, aesthetic, learned, forgiving, and kind.

The spirit in the room once again warmed, following Dan's lead. People regained animation, speaking with a fluid release of tension. I interrupted, wanting to capture the meaning of the exchange that had just happened, an exquisitely "teachable moment." I thanked Dan for the honor he'd shown his neighbors in expressing his feelings. I congratulated Darcy for her genuine desire to hear Dan and to understand. I talked about the more common experience people in oppressed identity groups so often encounter. Someone feels injured, as Dan had, and speaks the hurt. The listener, a person embedded in dominant cultural assumptions, is shocked, perhaps frightened, perhaps guilty, and, inadvertently, dismissive. "No, no, I didn't mean that." The speaker hears a sub-text: "You must be crazy! How could you possibly think that about me?!" The conversation switches from the pain of the person wronged to the hurt of the person who unconsciously caused harm. The "minority" person either assumes the role of caregiver, or, more commonly, falls silent in resentment and fatigue. The "dominant culture" person doesn't have an opportunity to learn something she cannot otherwise understand. Had Darcy reacted defensively, Dan might have sustained another in a long list of injuries and vowed never again to speak out in "mixed company." Once again, communication would have fallen apart, as it so often does.

This dynamic is one of the defining features of America's failure to get beyond our racial divide. As a white woman, I cannot know many things about the experience of people of a different status in society. I may not even know what it is I don't know. But I can know I *don't* know, and, like Darcy, I can want to know. Once given the opportunity to learn, I can signal openness by believing what I hear. If I do not do that, then the speaker is in triple jeopardy: not only must she take the risk of expressing emotion, but she must then prove the validity of what she is experiencing, and then she must overcome my resistant emotional reaction before she can be heard. Power imbalances in every one of the domains I delineated in the previous chapter are thus cast into permanency.

People listened to my comments with evident interest, and then resumed the conversation in process as Dan and others completed their tour of the original mural. Johanna spoke movingly about how the mural signified respect, acceptance, belonging—exactly the qualities that both Giulio and Brandon, speaking of entitlement and standing, had evoked in the first session. "Preserving the mural," she went on, "is a kind of code for the effort of people who are challenged by the changes happening in the neighborhood to stay and to continue having a significant presence."

Each of the remaining participants similarly elaborated their feelings and desires. For Susan it was respect for the process of creating the mural and for the artist who had led that project; for Monique an opportunity to reflect change. Michael wanted to see something that represented the new diversity of the community, interracial families for instance, while preserving the integrity of the building as much as possible. Finally, Mauricio made a powerful argument for the importance of the mural facing Cortland, a thoroughfare central to the community. But for the first time, he also spoke about the need to update the artwork, to reflect current reality as well as past.

The group drew collective breath. Into the moment of silence, Larry spoke. "I want to make a proposal: no mural on the front, but a WPA plaque. We could preserve the original mural inside the building, along with text explaining its meaning. And we could create new, updated murals on the back and side walls."

"Yes," said Dan enthusiastically. "We could compress the mural onto two sides of the building, and create a program for sustainability, so the mural isn't lost in the future."

## From Relationship-Building to Negotiation

I was frankly surprised. I was also moved, and more than a little worried. So much had happened in our two sessions that had opened people to disparate points of view. The emotional exchanges were deeply connecting, and the explorations of meanings embodied by the building and the artwork enlightening. But I had not anticipated that the group would be ready to begin solving the puzzle of a resolution, and certainly not so soon or without more preparation. Larry, I knew, was a leader and a unifier. That he made the first proposal made sense. That he made the particular proposal he made was bold. Dan's agreement and creative elaboration was a testimonial, I thought, to the heart-bonds that had grown in the course of the evening. But I also felt that agreement was premature. We had not yet dealt with deep enough levels of the conflict. Unaddressed, I feared they would bubble to the surface and undo any solution reached so quickly.

Nonetheless, a hum of agreement went round the room. And then Mauricio rose to his feet, moving toward the door. "I don't agree," he declared. "I'm not willing to talk about it tonight. It's late; we're at the end of the time we agreed to meet. I'm leaving!"

I (strenuously!) urged him to sit down and, as he did, agreed that we needed more time to move toward a solution, if the group now wanted to adopt that goal. Negotiations can take different forms. Generally, they can be classified as adversarial or cooperative. The first category is by far the more common in our society; clearly, I wanted any negotiation we did to be cooperative. And that took a strong commitment to the goal, some skill-building, and time—lots of time.

Were they willing to meet again? Yes, everyone agreed, they were willing to meet again, although willingness did not easily translate into scheduling. The library was due to reopen in five days. If we could come to a conclusion before then, the sigh of relief from city hall would be heard round the world! But there was no hope of finding a meeting time during the week. After some discussion, we agreed to reconvene the weekend after the opening.

As people collected their possessions and got ready to leave, Mauricio, who still seemed to me to be unsettled, spoke into the hum of conversation. "I'd like to meet somewhere else—not at Larry's, not at the library." The room stilled again. No one disagreed; the obvious other place to meet was the neighborhood center and Larry and Johanna promised to see whether a room would be available. I heard and noted Mauricio's sub-text: he was preparing a negotiation table with no tilts in any direction.

Before we parted, I strongly suggested that the participants use whatever strength and patience they had left to exchange some compliments. There was warmth and optimism in the room, but also alarm. I knew the conflict had changed substantially, but, as Mauricio's request reflected, conflict there still was aplenty. People had all worked so hard and genuinely that they deserved some verbal rewards as well as infusions of energy for the work that lay ahead. Someone thanked Mauricio for staying to the end; other "strokes" flowed among people.

# 6

# Negotiation

## *Swings and Crunches*

ONCE AGAIN, the time between meetings was productive. This time, I organized it. At the first meeting, I had grouped people with like positions. Now I proposed that small groups of people with conflicting positions get together to brainstorm alternative possibilities. I formed three groups of four, challenging people to work together with individuals from whom they were most distant. Their assignment was to come up with at least three visions of a way to settle the issue of the mural that would most encompass what they knew others wanted. In an email, I listed the elements I saw emerging as most crucial. Any solution would have to encompass all the qualities and concerns on my list:

> The next step is for smaller groupings of you to get together and exercise the imagination and goodwill I know you all bring to this process. Here's my attempt to synthesize the elements that are critical to members of the group:
> - Making a powerful statement in support of the history and cultures of Bernal folks, past, present & future
> - Acknowledging change in the community by expanding images to reflect new types of families
> - Acknowledging the fact that change has unequally affected different segments of the community
> - Honoring the contributions of the people who created both library and mural: the architect, the artist, the community members who took part with ideas and paintbrushes

- Capturing the major visual elements of the mural and the stories behind them
- Honoring the landmark quality of the library building
- Manifesting a presence in the neighborhood that expresses what an important resource the library is for the community
- Acknowledging the meaning and contributions of the WPA (and perhaps linking them with the needs of the moment)
- Proceeding in a way that embodies shared Bernal values of respect, multiculturalism, and progress

What have I missed? Please add to the list anything that seems crucial to you that I haven't captured here.

Two days later, on January 30, the renovated library reopened. It was a glorious event, celebrated with dancing and drums and speeches from city leaders. The line of residents waiting to see the renovation stretched literally around a long block—hundreds of people, many with children in strollers waiting with good-natured chatter for their chance to flow through the building and see what had been wrought. I had come down with a cold and laryngitis; lacking robust energy, I opted to mingle with the crowds rather than crowd my way indoors. Everything I heard reflected the way in which this library constituted an identity for the community. The people waiting were a rainbow representation of diversity on the hill. There was pride in the building, gratitude for the resources it offered, and relief that children's story hour would now be resuming after the months of hiatus.

What didn't happen was any kind of protest. The library staff had worried about that. I had consulted with Luis Herrera, the city librarian, and the local librarians about how they might answer questions about the mural and the mediation, and I had suggested that anxiety about a negative commotion was most likely unfounded. Although those who staunchly sought to protect the mural had not explicitly promised to abstain from demonstrating, my sense was that Mauricio was participating in the mediation in good faith (if also with some remaining caution) and that he recognized the wisdom of refraining from actions so provocative that they might further hostilities.

Two days after the opening, I received a phone call from the mayor's office. If the mediation succeeded in constructing a community consensus about new work on the library, the representative said, the mayor would offer strong support that any new work be funded. Hope, I thought, was reaching high places!

With these successes adding wind to our sails, the mediation group met again the next Saturday.

## Negotiation: Cooperative or Adversarial?

The Bernal group embodied many different oppositions: populist versus elite; Latino versus Anglo; old-timers versus newcomers; poor people versus affluent people; true San Francisco versus Silicon Valley; community art versus public art. The possibility that people might negotiate from entrenched positions was substantial. Typically, when negotiators feel little or no affinity for their opponents and are intent on defending rigid positions, the medium of negotiation becomes coercion: Who can deploy greater power to force the opponent to submit?

Cooperative negotiation, in contrast, relies on the ability of each participant to advocate equally for her own interests and for every other participant's. To do that, one needs to have a clear understanding of one's own underlying interests. If they are not well articulated, then it is easy to lapse into a need to insist on a particular position. Giulio knew that he felt resentful of newcomers' introduction to the neighborhood not because they had come to live there but because of ways they had behaved. He had experienced them as acting from a sense of entitlement to alter customs and relations to suit themselves. He may have started lobbying to restore the original mural, but his articulation of the roots of his feelings about neighborhood change enabled him to engage in a much more creative exploration of ways to reconstitute the art to reflect a spirit of community he missed.

At the same time that each participant needs to know herself with dimensionality, she also needs to feel camaraderie dimensional enough that she genuinely wishes all others involved in the negotiation also will end up happy. As the Bernal group engaged in deeply truthful discourse, expressing their experience of what had taken place with emotional honesty and in respectful language, they formed bonds that established shared interests in each other's well-being. Dan wanted Darcy to be cared for, and Darcy equally reciprocated.

These feelings of mutual regard are necessary underpinnings of cooperative negotiation. The reason for beginning with emotional dialogue is to build relationships of real and reciprocal regard that can sustain the spirit of simultaneous self-regard and concern for the other that structure the negotiation interaction.

When Roger Fisher and Bill Ury published *Getting to Yes* in 1981, they established a "canon" for principles of negotiation. A product of the Harvard Project on Negotiation, the book set forth three injunctions: negotiate from interests not positions; separate the people from the problem; and expand the pie. Much of what we had done in the first two sessions of the Bernal mediation was to voice the interests underlying people's positions. "Interests" is a word that evokes legal matters, which is not surprising given the business orientation of Fisher and Ury's work. Depending on the context in which the work takes place, language for articulating interests may take many narrative forms. For us, in the community and cultural context in which we worked, interests were expressed as personal recollections, historical stories, emotional accountings.

## Culture and Worldviews

The second of Ury and Fisher's principles became highly controversial as soon as their work was published. One feature by which we might characterize cultures is the degree of individualism on one end of the range, and of collectivism on the other. Socialization to an individualistic culture rests on assumptions about the value of independence from relationships beyond the nuclear family. These "boundaries" become internalized through a set of common beliefs about the hazards of public emotional expression. And indeed in a setting where competitive social relations are prevalent, personal revelation can become damaging. To learn reticence equips people to compete in a labor market lacking a social commitment to care for all people. At the same time, it shapes a set of interpersonal relations that undermine community and isolate individuals in domestic situations where labor is too scarce and resources inadequate.

In traditionally communitarian cultures, in contrast, extended family and neighbors are core to a sense of individual identity. In my classes, I often ask students how they identify themselves. "Anglo" students sometimes refer to gender, but more often they name a characteristic: athletic, kind, serious, a flake. Their peers, however, more often say Latina or African-American, Chinese or Filipino. Nomenclature links powerfully with worldviews, which are generationally transmitted and reinforced by experiences of discrimination. I was raised Jewish in a secular family living in a southern city where Jews were less than 1 percent of the population. We were seen by our peers, I believe, as exotic and somewhat unsavory outsiders. That daily experience layered on my consciousness of the Holocaust, which had taken place in the early years of my life. We all have multiple identities: gender, class, religion, region, physical ability, sexual orientation; each at different times can take a central position. At home or with other Jewish friends, I rarely experienced my primary identity in religious terms; I was the smart kid, the bad dancer, or something else more personal. But when I was at school and someone used an unwittingly anti-Semitic epithet, I became seriously Jewish in my mind. For people whose sense of self and way of ordering the world is deeply linked with a collective identity and the experience of living in community, separating people from problems is a wholly incomprehensible concept. It translates into a need to separate self from community and mind from emotion, to deny that which is most essentially self, a wrenching experience that often gives rise to escalated conflict.

To negotiate cooperatively requires, as I've said, an ability to hold self and other as equal in rights, or entitlement as Giulio expressed it, and power, or standing in Brandon's words. Having worked through wounds and perceptions that interfere with that ability, negotiators need next to shape the discourse in a way that operationalizes a spirit of mutual regard.

The first step is for each negotiator to speak fully exactly what she most wants as the outcome. Conventionally, we often begin negotiating in one of two ways: we either exaggerate our objective or we minimize it. In the first case, we are betting that the "other side" will do the same thing. If we each ask for 120 percent of what we really want, then we'll have room to horse trade, sacrificing 20 percent and ending up with perfection. In the meantime, however, we breed bad feeling in the relationship. In the second case, we may feel unentitled to what we want, or worried about doing harm to the other person. We therefore begin by asking for 80 percent of what we want. Once we've negotiated and given up some more, we end up with 60 percent, too little for any sustainable sense of satisfaction, and once again the relationship is damaged.

I began the third meeting of the Bernal group by asking each individual to say what he or she truly wanted to see happen. As the conversation moved around the table (we literally sat at a table in a small meeting room at the Neighborhood Center), each person spoke of the vision produced in dialogue with other members of their small group. These expressions echoed the group statements in the first meeting, but now were very different. Amy led off. At the start, she had argued for no artwork on the library; now she called for moving forward on a public art process. She imagined a quilt of strong images that respected the lines of the building, of permanent and temporary areas and artwork spilling over to other public spaces around the library.

Michael, Dan, and Darcy focused on the use of mosaic tiles, all equally excited about the vision of the mural reinterpreted in a different, more durable medium.

Brandon also spoke of recreating the mural in a new form, introducing the idea of statuary in places where the façade did not invite "art on the wall." His group had concentrated on qualities, primarily of respect for a variety of aesthetics and for producing in the end a work of truly good art.

Finally, Mauricio, who had listened quietly until now, spoke of ownership. He explained that what mattered most to him was that people of color in the community felt the work reflected them and their experience. Wise in the realities of fund-raising, he brought money into the conversation, urging the group to stay focused on a mural first lest funds not be adequate to do all the wonderful art-making we were imagining.

And then he joined the expansive spirit in the room and led directly to Ury and Fisher's third injunction, to expand the pie: "What about the fourth wall?" he asked. "Why should we be limited only to the original three?"

## How to Craft a Consensus

Each negotiator having defined the ideal outcome, "asking for 100 percent of what I want," the next step is to identify the differences and then to work them out in a way that equally takes care of each person. Naming differences is the job of the mediator. Often, by this time in a conflict intervention, everyone has a desire to gloss over differences. There is good-will in the room. People lean toward agreement. That momentum is a wonderful thing—but it is a mistake. The mediator needs to articulate clearly every detail of disagreement she detects, for these points are the content of the negotiation to come. Anything missed at this stage is likely to rear up later to bite the process. To be sure, it is wise also to identify areas of agreement, but even more important to say courageously, "Here are the differences we need to work through to the point of agreement." In the Bernal case, I heard that the group was zeroing in on an agreement to make new artwork. I also heard assumptions about how much of the original mural would be preserved, how much clear wall reclaimed. There were questions implied about the kind of artwork, and a very meaningful debate about who would make the new work: any member of the community who wished to take part, or professional artists engaging the community's ideas but free to make their own interpretation and implementation? Was this, in the words of Susan and Amy, both artists and representing the clearest polarization on this question, to be community art or public art?

With all these issues on the table, we set about to work them through. I think about the next steps as a sequence of explorations:

First, dream big: brainstorm solutions that give everyone 150 percent. That is, what new ideas, stimulated by a new calculus of expanded resources, might produce an outcome better than anyone had imagined? The mayor's offer of funding helped stimulate the Bernal group to think about more walls, more grounds, more forms, more mediums.

If that doesn't resolve the issue, then explore common ground: using "both—and" rather than "either—or" thinking, can we find a way to take care of everyone's needs? As long as we were thinking about the entire campus of the library, the possibilities for having clean walls and painted walls were real. The stickler, though, was the significance of one particular wall, the Cortland façade. There was no way to have both a clear and a decorated wall there. In my experience mediating, it's rare to find a genuinely zero-sum problem, but this dispute had the potential to be one.

Next, look for compromises that do the least injustice to anyone's interests and are equally shared. Giving up a little bit of the wall or a little bit of the mural was possible but didn't really solve anything. Nobody would be satisfied. This solution was in fact a version of the one proposed by the Library Commission. It had recommended that the mural be reproduced on the Cortland side and eliminated on the other two sides. Nobody had been happy.

At this point, the negotiators might have to face the reality that someone will sacrifice more than someone else. If that sacrifice is too great, however, whatever agreement is reached will not hold. The crafting of this step depends, therefore, heavily on the spirit in which it is done. Compassion and gratitude go a long way. Because of the moving and culturally-compelling way that members of the Bernal group had spoken of meanings the mural held for them, people who had started out determined to have no artwork on the library were now very much more open to a different outcome. Most of us have a strong desire to see justice done in the worlds we inhabit. The "newcomers" in the Bernal group had comprehended on a visceral level how the "old-timers" experienced changes to the community as unjust. That new understanding, interwoven with the humanly emotional ways in which it had been communicated, compelled change in the wishes of the no-mural representatives. It was not that they wanted to please the others, but instead that their interests had come to overlap significantly with the interests of the other segment of the group. Similarly, the Save the Bernal Library Mural people now saw the others as humans, with value to their aesthetic and historical vision. In the balance, the will of the group now tilted in the direction of some forms of new art on and around the building.

If one "side" bends more in the direction of the other, what forms of compensation might they receive? Equalizing the costs if not the benefits of a solution helps to construct a durable agreement. In our case, the "no mural" people were facing a harder task to carry their "constituents" along with a solution involving something on the Cortland façade than the "save the mural" folks. Could the latter help the former in that process? Could the agreement include a commitment to a blending of aesthetic approaches that might help to engage the clean walls people in the creative process?

Finally, every agreement is a work in progress. Having concluded an arduous negotiation, people generally want to celebrate, not recalibrate. But an essential part of any consensus is the knowledge that it can and should be renegotiated if it doesn't hold up in the real world. What good is an agreement that binds people to something they really don't want to do? For me, the point is to strengthen relationships among people in a spirit of justice and progress. Resentment for being bound to an agreement that doesn't serve those ends is counterproductive. Agreements need to be living things, changing as people and circumstances change, responsive to human needs rather than procedurally binding.

## Untying Tight Knots

One of the assignments a mediator takes on is courage. After the Bernal group poured out vision and creativity and affection, it fell to me to say the hard words: *Cortland façade.* I knew that the reality was that we still had hard work facing us. Immediately, tension returned to the room. Voices, a moment before filled with laughter and excitement, now tightened.

Also, for better or for worse, the clock was running out. We had vowed to respect time limits we had set as a group. Now, it was late and we had very few minutes left. I proposed the obvious: we need to meet again. So far, it had been miraculously easy to find times to meet. A group of fifteen people, all with uncommonly busy schedules, had agreed on three appointments in a two-week span, an exquisite act of dedication. Now, however, in the clinch, hearts faltered and calendars intruded. We could not agree on a meeting time.

So we ended with what had become a ritual of closure—speaking our appreciation for each other—and my promise that I'd contact everyone and find the next confluence.

# 7

# Documents and Disturbances

*Negotiating in the Real World*

IT TOOK TEN DAYS to reach consensus on a meeting time. I interpreted the difficulty of that process as a warning sign of impending burn-out. People were feeling, I thought, both tired and anxious. Although the group had already exceeded my expectations for the mediation by striving for a negotiated settlement, I sensed that few if any of them actually saw a way that might come to pass.

At length, we determined to meet again at the Neighborhood Center on the evening of February 16. Following the strong convergences that had happened in the last two meetings, my intuitive sense was that the participants were now pulling away, driven by a kind of centrifugal energy born of anxiety. Concerned people not at the table were daily expressing more concern. I was getting emails and copies of replies to emails voicing heated opinions and questioning how much longer the suspense would last before a decision was known.

## Things that Go Bump in the Night

In any mediation dealing with public issues, there are ghosts at the table. (Indeed, the same can be said about most "private" mediations, too!) Depending on the importance of the issue to the public, the number and significance of the ghosts multiplies. Two more or less organized constituencies had all along been a presence and now began to declare themselves more loudly.

Between the first and second mediation sessions, Mauricio had discovered the organizing potential of Facebook. One of his fellow

Save the Bernal Library Mural committee members had established a page and invited participation. Over a couple of weeks, several hundred people signed on. Mauricio expressed fascination—and excitement—about this new tool. Predictably, neighbors who disagreed with the website's position were upset about its existence. I had talked with Mauricio, Darcy, and several other mediatees about the question. My feeling was mild; it might serve the process we were conducting better to do less agitation in the community outside the room, but I understood Mauricio's inclination to make manifest the strength of his constituency. During the second meeting, the Facebook page was addressed in the form of "held feelings" and *paranoias*. The page cast doubt on Mauricio's seriousness in negotiating in a genuinely cooperative spirit. Several other organizing activities had added to the concern. Mauricio's group had held a fund-raising party at a popular Latino club on Mission Street. Dan had printed up posters and the group had distributed them to storefronts around the neighborhood. All in all, it was clear that Mauricio had no intention of calling off his campaign while negotiations proceeded.

But did those actions mean he also had no real intention to negotiate in good faith? I had several long talks with Mauricio and urged him to explain his motivations to the group, which he did in response to Darcy's questions. The poorer, Latino and Filipino segments of the community, he said, had too often experienced disadvantage. There was a prevalent anticipation of being overlooked and overridden. Successful negotiation depended on a sense of strength, not weakness. To make manifest the numbers supporting his position was to put him in a position to negotiate as an equal, an essential precondition to an outcome that would stand the test of time.

My contribution to the controversy was to theorize the significance of equalizing power to the process we were undertaking. At the same time, I urged Mauricio to conduct his campaign with respect for his opponents. If those who disagreed with him were vilified in public discourse, then the ability of the group to form and sustain the interconnected relationships necessary to successful negotiation would be damaged. Mauricio had heard enough reflection of how hurtful some of his earlier rhetoric had been that he agreed; the tone of the campaign did in fact grow noticeably more celebratory, less laced with name-calling or judgment.

Now, a week after the third session, with tensions once again rising, Darcy launched a counter Facebook page. I knew that there had been roiling commentary within her group of neighbors. Amy had done a thorough and skillful job of answering emailed questions from members of the "New Deal for Bernal" group (with the subject line "Inquiring Minds Want to Know"). She wrote careful summaries of what was happening in the mediation, while urging people to wait patiently. Darcy was experiencing a growing dilemma in her more casual interactions with no-mural folks. Her store was a sort of town center on Cortland Avenue. People dropped in to shop her whimsical and beautiful stock, and also to chat with Darcy. She had, in fact, been dubbed the Mayor of Cortland Avenue, for she performed a valued role as a nurturer of community. She had drawn thunder early in the library controversy when she posted in her window a petition calling for the removal of the mural, characterizing the artwork uncharitably. Darcy had long since apologized for that action, and now was in a process of changing as her understanding of what the mural meant to Giulio and Dan and others grew vivid. How was she to communicate her shifting feelings to angry neighbors who dropped by to express themselves in the course of a business day?

One way to think about the dynamics we were experiencing is in terms of the relationship between identity and association. Each individual in the mediation was undergoing a shift of identity. I've pointed out how many different identities we each entertain at any moment; the particular one (or ones) that assume centrality depend very much on the social circumstances of the moment. So identity is both deeply intrinsic to a sense of self, and at the same time highly situational.

In the course of the mediation, the people at the table were forming new identities as members of the mediation group itself. Key to that new sensibility was a shared determination to solve the problem of the library mural. And that shared purpose was reinforced by the amount of time we were spending together as well as the intensity of the emotional exchanges. Learning together, sharing that extraordinarily elating experience of changing ideas about the world together, moving through animosity to affection, all reinforced and deepened the growing of a new group identity.

But for the people not at the table, none of those experiences was taking place. They were dependent on secondhand reporting from Mauricio and Darcy and Amy and others. No doubt, every individual in the mediation worked a good deal of persuasive magic in communicating to their peers, but the levels of change taking place were not equivalent. These concerned onlookers still were grounded in association with their original cohorts. They were denied the opportunity to engage the "other" and to learn and change from that encounter. So far, we had consciously declined to extend the consensus-building work to the larger community, judging that the time for that needed to await a viable consensus by the smaller group.

### Laboring at the Table and in the Street

And so each member of the mediation was tasked with acting as an organizer in her or his own circle. Community organizing theory may lay out campaigns as orderly steps in a rationalized process. But in reality, organizing just as often happens in quick conversations in stores and cafés and passing greetings on the street. Elsewhere, I've theorized the ways in which we form ideas about the world, seeing that process happening in three realms simultaneously: from personally lived experience, from interactions in community, and from more distant sources (Roy 1994). Both Darcy and Mauricio lived and breathed in the second realm (as did everyone else, albeit perhaps with less intensity). In their daily interactions, they were attitude influencers. But influencing attitudes seated in passionately held oppositions is a difficult process. Darcy, like Mauricio, exercised influence not by her position but by the vibrant force of her personality. She is wholly transparent, joyful, fun, and also thoughtfully well-considered. At this stage of the mediation, she began slowing down her brief exchanges with members of her cohort, telling people in more detail what changes were occurring for her and how she hoped they would come along.

But the New Deal people were understandably nervous. They perceived "their side" as having respected the mediation process by holding their public campaign in abeyance. But Mauricio's "side" was not being similarly discreet. Darcy's new Facebook page was therefore both a tool for addressing her constituency's concerns and a political act manifesting the group's willingness to meet Mauricio on oppositional as well as cooperative terms. It said, politely but definitively, we will not simply fade away.

So negotiation stances were forming in two realms (at least!) in which power was operating: at the table through relationship-building and in the community through both face-to-face interaction and public campaigning. To me, that was all part of the process, but it required of me some work in support of the organizing the mediatees were doing on a daily basis. I continued my conversations with Mauricio and at the same time offered to meet with a group of New Dealers. We had a good conversation in which I answered many of their questions and talked through with them the framework in which we were working. I also offered them appreciation for the difficulty of their position; passivity was clearly not their preferred way to behave, but they had agreed—and now recommitted to—waiting to see what their neighbors wrought with as much patience as they could muster. I offered to speak with them again if they needed more updating or help keeping faith with the process.

Meanwhile, things were shifting in another domain of power as well. I was getting multiple expressions of support, and of concern, from officials in the city. Now and then, I'd receive an emailed inquiry about how things were going. I tried to remember, in the press of work, to drop a note to the directors of the two commissions that were potentially the final decision-makers, the library and arts commissions. David Campos continued to attend meetings; I believe he missed one evening because of an emergency board meeting (the San Francisco City Council). Otherwise, he sat through every minute, very occasionally offering encouragement or information, but mostly listening in an attitude of respectful support. He kept the mayor's office informed, consciously building support of a more political and material kind as we went along.

What these links to the world of official power provided was a sense of possibility. Sometimes public policy processes invite citizen participation but in the end fail to satisfy the wishes of people who have become involved. It is one thing to have no voice as decisions are made, and quite another to give voice and end up feeling overlooked and powerless. While the directors had assured me going into the mediation that they would support any decision that came from the community, their ongoing interest signaled that they really meant it. I believe everyone in the mediation group understood that, on some level, we were engaged in a political process and that there was no guarantee our conclusion would prevail. But we all needed to be able to make a reasonable assessment that our consensus, should we reach one, would have significant influence. Energy to devote the time, thought, emotion, and creativity to the process would not otherwise be forthcoming.

On Feb. 16, David convened a meeting in his city hall office with the two directors, two members of each commission, and two of us engaged in the mediation (another representative couldn't attend at the last minute). We reported on our progress and gained more official—but still provisional—assurances of support. The officials also sorted out lines of decision-making authority and began to sketch procedures for moving a final plan through the process. Finally, commission members suggested means of supporting ultimate implementation of a new art-making process.

## Putting It in Writing

Timing and momentum are equally important factors. In describing the aftermath of successfully concluded conflict intervention, my good friend Roberto Chené coined the phrase, "tendency to revert to the status quo ante." As the time lengthened before our next meeting, I worried that we were experiencing just that. The Facebook pages redefined polarities, however carefully Darcy crafted her content to be conciliatory. There was in reality a competition to see whose page accrued more "friends." Mauricio was becoming increasingly enchanted with the organizing capacity of the Internet, thinking ahead to the next campaign for a good cause and the next one after that. Looking to the future of community empowerment shifted his gaze from the present negotiation to future possibilities.

Meanwhile, we had attracted the notice of the press. Several brief articles about the mediation appeared in both English- and Spanish-language papers. In each, either Mauricio or Darcy was quoted, and neither could be said to be entirely unbiased. We had failed to make a plan in advance to deal with the media, an oversight that taught me a lesson. The fall-out was not severe, but it did spark a few "Held Feelings." Overall, I thought the reportage to be helpful, because it spoke in the larger context of the city to the seriousness of what we were doing. Later, when we had finally come to a conclusion, the reporting was supportive and helpful.

At this stage, though, I felt the need to refocus the group's attention by drafting a statement of consensus that I thought captured the spirit of where we had been in the last meeting. On February 16, a week before we were next to meet, I emailed the draft to everyone and invited their comments. After congratulating them on our having finally arrived at a meeting time the following week, I wrote:

> I've been talking with many of you, as well as folks from the extended community. Based on our sessions and on those conversations, I've drafted a document that begins to frame a statement of consensus. I'm attaching it here. Will each of you look it over and let me know what you think: Are you in sufficient agreement with it to be willing to move on to constructing a community art project? If not, what would you change?
>
> Before we meet, I'd like to engage each of you in the process of crafting the statement so that we can complete the consensus process when we meet. Our next—and final—task will be to create a means to carry that consensus out into the larger community.

I can't tell you how much I respect the integrity, honesty and creativity you've each brought to this work! We're in the home stretch.

It turned out that my projection of completing the work in the next meeting was overly optimistic. I've included the first draft statement in Appendix C. It was to undergo many, many revisions before we were done.

# 8

# Consensus! . . . and Disruption

NOW BEGAN an arduous process of negotiation and word-smithing. Tempers flared and calmed like the San Francisco weather. Daily, pressure to be finished swelled. Voices in the community reached us in a punctuated rhythm: What's happening? Why the delay? What can we expect? On the political front, rumors amassed that our very supportive mayor might run for governor or other state office. He might soon be gone; would his successor feel as friendly toward our work?

Time is a crucial and often-overlooked force in any conflict process. Time scarcity increases conflict; in mediation, it equally closes down space for good feeling and encourages polarization. Many mediations conducted in today's world do not have the luxury of sufficient time. Courts await outcomes, clocks tick away expensive minutes, business dealings hang in the balance. I have known mediations to force conclusions that were enormously injurious to people because the mediator needed to produce results for an evaluating supervisor when parties were too emotionally fraught and too inadequately supported to insist on a viable outcome. One battered woman in my practice, a stay-at-home mother, finally called the police when her husband tried to hit her with a two-by-four in front of their three children. While he was (briefly) jailed, she left with the kids. Soon after, the couple went to mediation to make an urgent interim financial agreement, but her husband refused to negotiate unless she apologized for humiliating him in front of their children and the neighbors. She refused to give him an apology; he refused to discuss anything without it. The mediator, an employee in a for-profit agency, had limited time to meet. She urged the woman to make some sort of apology, and when my client wouldn't, in the last few minutes the mediator rushed through an agreement that left the divorcing wife without enough money to feed herself and the children, who remained in her custody. My client left the meeting in shock, not sure how it had happened but determined not to trade her dignity even for necessary financial support.

While that example was extreme, the dynamic is common. Truly consensual negotiation, as I've written earlier, requires enough time to work through relationship breaches in a real way. Otherwise, negotiation becomes adversarial. There is research suggesting how importantly cultural factors impact non-collaborative negotiation. Those with an eye to future good feeling often sacrifice the will to win and compromise while the adversary stays fixed determinedly to a goal. Women, and more generally people from more communitarian cultures—often people of color—end up with less satisfactory settlements.

I feared that we might devolve into another version of the time-bind dilemma. I found myself in contradictory roles: on the one hand I held back the tide of urgency, and on the other I urged the group to keep moving toward conclusion.

## Getting Done

When I mediate, I take notes. As a private practitioner, I'm not required to document my work, but I find note-taking to be helpful. Not only do I have a record to support my memory later, but charting the things people say as they say them helps me to be sure I've understood what they are saying. It also gives me a visual representation of the flow of communication, providing a crude representation of whether each individual has had sufficient opportunity to speak and how the emotional tenor of the dialogue is moving in the room.

For the fourth session of the Bernal mediation, my notes fail. Shortly before the meeting, Johanna called me for help formulating some feelings she was having about Mauricio and his campaign. She had caught a radio broadcast of an interview with him and others from his Save the Bernal Library Mural group. She was upset at what seemed to her to be a misrepresentation of the process we were in, as well as some harsh rhetoric she feared would rekindle flames of opposition just as we were coming together to craft a shared solution. I supported her to speak her mind and coached her to formulate what she felt in the forms I had taught. When we gathered at the neighborhood center the evening of February 24, Johanna opened the dialogue by addressing Mauricio with her "held feelings" and *paranoias*.[1] Mauricio heard her respectfully, demurring that the sharpest rhetoric had come not from him but from others in his group. Brandon joined the conversation with his *paranoia* that it nonetheless represented what Mauricio thought. Mauricio validated that such language once might have come from him but he was seeing the value of a nonabrasive approach. What was true, however, was that, as we approached consensus, he was uncertain how to turn the organizing campaign he had initiated in the direction of collaborative problem solving. He suggested it was a bit too soon; his people needed more tangible evidence that their voices were in fact being heard before they'd be willing to lower the volume. With all the sweetness and authority at his command, Larry urged Mauricio to accept both the influence he had on his community and the responsibility to use it to support the mediation process.

Once again, this pivotal exchange helped focus the group's good will on crafting a viable solution, helping to convince people that Mauricio was indeed on board. Terry led off the discussion. He had come into the mediation grounded in his knowledge of the library's history and wishing it restored to the WPA façade. Now, however, he declared full support for the direction we were taking, looking forward with an historian's eye to making new art. "What we have here," he said, "is an opportunity to do a significant event in the neighborhood. This is the time people will look back to fifty years from now, just as we look back fifty years to the original painting."

Giulio, who had spoken so vividly for the restoration of the mural, now said, "The library's history is so much about struggle. In the new work, we can incorporate the WPA struggle as well."

1. For a discussion of the radical therapy usage of the word *paranoia*, see chap. 12, n.1.

Each person spoke in turn about their hopes for the new work. People imagined plazas reaching to the recreation center, improvements to the playground, and more. With the keen eye of a practical visionary, Mauricio again refocused the discussion on the library walls.

I very much appreciated the spirit of the meeting. Clearly, every individual in the room leaned toward a creative conclusion. But I knew that there were still major disagreements, as well. We had formed a direction in theory, but we still had not truly come to agreement about the thorniest issue: the Cortland wall. Now, as we began to craft the final details of the agreement, I once again named that elephant in the room. I worried that the waves of good feeling might sweep people into an agreement that hadn't deeply enough addressed the conflict. That was the dynamic that had happened at the end of the second session, and I could well imagine it's happening again now. I wanted people to look squarely into the face of division and emerge with a stronger consensus.

The group rolled up their collective sleeves and proceeded to take my draft statement apart, line by line. Now and then the discussion stalled on a particular point: On a range from restoring the mural to eliminating it, where should we fall? Would the walls end up mostly bare with a few pale remnants of what was now there? Or would we reproduce the current mural, only in a smaller scale that better respected the architecture? Each time we hit one of those hard disagreements, someone—often Michael or Monique, the two participants least fixed in a position and therefore most able to access creative new ideas—suggested something that reopened the sense of possibility and re-engaged the group in collaboration. Michael, for instance, fantasized free-standing objects illuminated at night, perhaps even with changing images projected in space. Monique nudged the discourse away from old-timers and newcomers, or Anglos and Latinos, reminding us of all the young uncategorizable people in the community who were not well described by those terms: same-sex families, multiracial couples, returned descendants of generations-old residents. As we proceeded, we changed words, substituting, for instance, "Revitalizing the Mural" for "Updating the Mural." We adjusted the emphasis to focus on meanings of the work and the process by which it would be produced, resisting our own creative imaginings of the artwork itself. "Leave the artwork to the artists" became the motto of the group, even though it was difficult to restrain the flow of creativity released by our process. Finally, we all agreed that the consensus statement should end by quoting the statement Terry had made at the beginning of the evening: we were making history right along with art.

The next day, Amy emailed her contacts in the community:

> Hopefully, with most everyone seeming more flexible about what MUST happen to this one facade (Cortland), the "two sides" are having a rapprochement. It has been fascinating to experience that which began as two fairly well delineated opposing sides . . . morph[ing] into a pretty good roundtable of folks being honest with very tough questions and issues, i.e., "how we have benefitted from gentrification." People have been speaking and hearing each other about things perhaps even more central to the crux of the divide—beyond mural esthetics—which was/is the feeling and passion about class, race, change, gentrification and how grey all of that really is. My concern is that one building's facade is a small canvas on which to project and esthetically resolve all of these issues. These discussions, tough as they can be, delineate a local version and microcosm of contemporary concerns that artwork and this type of community process can ameliorate.
>
> Wishing it was resolved, it is getting closer. Amy

Because time was short and lives busy, we designated a committee to produce the next draft of the statement. Brandon, Susan, Dan, Darcy and I met the following week. Once again, we went over the document in detail, incorporating the changes as we understood them from the last meeting. When we sent to the larger group this latest revision (the fourth, according to my document numbering system!), I summarized the committee's discussion:

We recognized in particular two areas of continuing disagreement:
- Which art-making process we'll use: art made by community members themselves, or art made by an artist informed by community members.
- What will ultimately end up on the Cortland façade, with a range of wishes from the majority of the current elements, to little or nothing with the crucial elements occurring on new free-standing objects.

On the first question, Susan suggested that the two approaches can be integrated. The issue becomes one of reliably selecting artistic leadership who will respect the community's sensibilities about the images and meanings of the existing mural, solicit new images that reflect changes in the community, and bring it all together with aesthetic integrity pleasing to as many people as humanly possible. The issue for us therefore becomes one of the selection process for the leading artist or artists. Bullet no. 3 addresses that process.

On the second question, in bullet no. 6 we made the quantities of mural and wall space a bit more concrete, and again referred to a design process rather than going too far into the realm of design ourselves.

If at this point you have reservations about signing onto the agreement—and even more, carrying our work out to the community members in your circle to elicit their agreement and participation—let me know right away, please! We'll then arrange a meeting with the committee to take further steps to address your concerns.

Optimistically, we'd like to convene a final meeting of the whole group at the earliest possible time, to plan the next steps—community inclusion, artist selection, negotiation with the city, etc.—and to celebrate our good work!

That email went out on March 2. I felt truly gratified about our progress, confident that we had only to dot a few remaining i's and cross a few t's. My complacency survived for about an hour. My phone rang. A neighbor asked, "What's the story on the Andover wall?" . . . and I realized new trouble was ringing our door-bell.

## Getting Undone

The Andover wall was a tall, long retaining wall that ran along the west side of the library down Andover street all the way to the recreation center. Years earlier, a local artist had painted a charming depiction of life on Bernal Hill, including portraits of the neighborhood "heroes," leaders who had made prominent contributions to the community. Giulio's father was on that wall, as was a beloved priest from the Catholic church on Cortland Avenue. Mauricio, who had commissioned and funded the Andover mural when he directed the neighborhood center, was also on the wall.

It didn't take long for me to learn that the artist who had painted the mural had just painted it out.

Josef Norris was one of the artists with whom I had consulted a few weeks earlier. For a laundry list of reasons, he had advocated the removal of the library mural. For technical reasons, he argued, it was impossible to truly restore it; it would have to be removed and repainted anyway. Painted murals were no longer tenable. They require too much maintenance and the city had established a policy of refusing to fund maintenance, or to support new public art that required it. The building was delicate and had never been a good canvas for a mural. The topic of his painting on the retaining wall had not come up. But I knew that it was deteriorating. The retaining wall, which was technically not attached to the library because it sat on recreation center property, had been seeping moisture for years. I had always found the flaking paint part of the work's charm, especially since enough of it remained vivid successfully to enchant.

I called Josef as soon as I heard the news. It was clear I was distressed. He explained that, as an artist, he hated to see his work in disrepair. He had learned that repainting the mural was not feasible—in fact, there was some indication the wall needed to be rebuilt at some near time in the future. He insisted he had consulted with no one about removing the art, that he had full rights to it and removal was his to do.

"But did you have to do it right now!?" I exclaimed. "The mediation is just at the point of consensus. This is going to stir up all kinds of controversy again!" I knew suspicions would tromp wildly through the community; I was already hearing them. On one side, those who wanted the library mural protected worried that "clean wall-ers," emboldened by the Andover example, were planning to take unilateral action to erase the library mural in a similar way. Josef had been known to argue in favor of removing the library mural. His view of community art was that it was a living manifestation of a moment in history. It needed to change as community changed. So some of the save-the-mural folks saw his action as a threat to their cause, an invitation to people to take paintbrushes in hand and settle the matter. On the other side, a neighbor stopped me on the street to claim that Josef's action was a provocative act intended to mobilize people to *save* the library mural, because he demonstrated how a revered artwork could vanish in a flash, without discussion. We were so near agreement; Josef's timing could not be worse!

I said all this to Josef. He was apologetic. I asked him to write something explaining his actions and to post it on the wall, and I also told him the mediation group was planning to write something about it, too. He agreed with alacrity.

Just as I feared, the disappearance of the Andover mural stimulated a flare-up of hostilities. Facebook rhetoric ratcheted up. Mauricio was outraged and said so very loudly. Emails flew among our mediation participants. Paradoxically, Josef's action eventually served to reunite the group: everyone was horrified. By the next afternoon, Josef had posted a statement along the wall, justifying his actions based on his rights to the work as its creator. He disclaimed a need to consult the community about "his" mural's destruction, explaining his actions entirely in terms of the deterioration of the wall and with it the images. It took our group a little over a week, many conversations, and an elaborate conference call, but in the end it helped us clarify our purposes, and we determined to use the event as a constructive moment. We wrote our own statement for the community, reflecting our growing unity and our commitment to collaborative process. We articulated clearly the concept of public art as a dialogue between artist and public, not the exclusive property of either. By contrast with how unilaterally the Andover business had come down, we described the thoughtful and time-consuming manner in which we were striving for agreement about something that, in the beginning, seemed irreconcilable precisely because it held so many meanings to people. The statement appears in Appendix D.

In any intervention involving people who are not actually present in the room, conflict is likely to be played out in a variety of forms outside the room. Whatever Josef's motivation, his action had symbolic and political meaning for many others. It therefore became a factor in the conflict, and in the intervention we were conducting. My role was to keep open the possibility that even such challenging events could be turned to good purpose. There is a particular philosophy underlying my own openness to that view. However shocked and worried I was by the news of the disappearance of the Andover mural at just that point, some part of my mind entertained the belief that people can learn new ways to regard a matter if helped to see it in a constructive framework. Like life, conflict is a dynamic phenomenon. Everything changes all the time. When Josef took up his paintbrush, he drew out the worst fears of people on all sides of the controversy. Once expressed, these stories of double-dealing and bad intentions can be addressed directly. Something in them is inevitably true; once that truth is acknowledged, the distortions surrounding it can be dispelled. That is what we sought to do in our written statement to the community, and by returning to our work at hand, the negotiation of a consensus.

**Back to the Table—and Forward to the Drawing Board**

And so the group returned to line-by-line revisions of the statement. The written document focused the work and broadened the terms of discussion. Several combinations of people revised it according to their goals; we compared these versions, seeing much confluence and defining all the more clearly where the conflict still lay. We scheduled a fifth session for March 17.

But one more event was to challenge our process.

At the center of Cortland Avenue, across the street from the library, there is a parking lot for the local upscale grocery store. Parked cars face a large billboard, the only such advertising space on the street. The day before we were to meet, a sign appeared on the billboard. Emblazoned with the slogan "Save the Bernal Library Mural," it replicated storefront posters that had circulated on the street for some time showing the original mural. Once again, my phone and email lit up. In addition to the boldness of the image itself, two other factors agitated the community: the billboard advertised a link to Precita Eye's website for more information about the mural controversy, and word spread of a fundraiser the coming weekend for the "Save the Bernal Library Mural" group. Again, even as Mauricio actively participated in email trails crafting revisions to the mediation's consensus statement, people at the table as well as others anxiously awaiting our final product raised doubts about Mauricio's commitment to supporting the outcome. Would the consensus be strong enough that Mauricio would turn his organizing energies to enlisting willing adherence from his followers? Would Darcy, Amy, and other "representatives" of the clean-walls folks be able to say with enough truthfulness that all segments of the community were united behind our proposed resolution? Tensions were high, only slightly relieved by an email exchange between Darcy and Mauricio early on the day of the meeting. Darcy had asked for help explaining the billboard and the fundraiser to "her folks." Mauricio replied at length, reiterating his intention to conduct an "educational and visibility campaign" parallel to the mediation process. "We're consciousness raising and building another voice in our community," he concluded.

Despite all that, when we gathered at the neighborhood center that night, the work went smoothly. We easily identified the points still in contention, discussing them with a clearly unanimous will to find solutions that addressed every concern. By the end of the meeting, we were elated: we had done it! We celebrated a bit and, tired but triumphant, we parted with hugs.

Triumph lasted until mid-afternoon the next day when my phone rang.

## On Second Thoughts and Better Agreements

Amy, Michael, and Terry had been talking with each other. Each woke up in the morning with disquiet. On waves of enthusiasm the night before, they had failed to voice remaining unease with some of the solutions we'd constructed. They did not want to sign on to the agreement. They offered to simply remove their names and let it go forward, but I rejected that possibility. Consensus meant everyone; if they were not truly in agreement, consensus meant more effort to work through their concerns and come up with better solutions.

We had arrived at a moment that can make or break a mediated process. When the relationship-building work of mediation has been powerfully experienced, there develops a strong momentum toward agreement. I believe this phenomenon is something very basic to the human condition. Despite the many social forces that result in divisions and hostilities, given half a chance we want to come together. We are social animals and, at our best, of good heart for each other. It is therefore very common that people make agreements at the moment of decision that may not reflect their interests thoroughly enough. On reflection, consensus weakens and eventually fails.

I was truly glad Amy called me the very next day. A lot of damage might have been done had the consensus statement gone out widely to the community (it had already been posted on Darcy's Facebook page) and then later revised. Fatigue nipping the edges of my heart, I nonetheless congratulated her on coming forward. I always tell people I work with that every agreement is a work in progress. It needs to be tested in the light of day, and possibly in practice as time goes on. Every agreement, therefore, needs to be a living artifact, made to be changed. The point is that people agree not to change agreements unilaterally. If a mediatee needs revisions, then they need to say so; in return, everyone must be ready to reengage that process.

And so I urged Amy to consult with Terry, Michael, and anyone else who was not happy and propose a new draft. She willingly agreed. By March 21, a new version was ready to circulate among the group. In the first rounds of producing the document, we had struggled with a particular point of tension: on the one hand, we wanted to leave as much of the design process for new artwork to the artists. So we focused on principles defining the work and a process for producing it. On the other hand, we also wanted to be as concrete as we could be in an effort to reassure the community that there would be a viable balance point between reinterpretations of the most prized old images and placement of artwork that significantly better honored the architecture of the building. In the end, we had come up with a percentage of the Cortland façade on which work would appear. Quantification of such intangible elements is very, very tricky, and it was primarily this number that had failed the test of even so short a time.

There were two other points that still needed work. During the discussions there had been many creative imaginings of forms of art that were not murals. Now, those wanting revisions suggested substituting the word "artwork" for mural, and perhaps specifically mentioning the possibility of other forms. Secondly, they were uneasy about any vagueness in describing the process by which artists would be hired to do the work.

For several days, emails circulated within the group and conversations went on among smaller groups of people. Tempers flared from time to time—and people continued talking with each other, working through dissension without my involvement. It was probably a good thing that I had a project to do out of town right after the work reopened. I urged people to accept that we were not done, that it was necessary to do one more round of negotiation—and then left them to begin to do it. My hope in mediating conflict is always that participants learn skills that enable them to better deal with conflict without intervention; I could see that was happening right now. Nonetheless, spirits were flagging. A proposal was made that two statements be circulated, sort of majority and minority reports. Several people quickly nixed that idea: we had come so far toward agreement that most of us were unwilling to give up with anything less than unanimity.

Email and other electronic media are helpful tools in conducting group process, but they have severe limitations. When feelings run hot, email is a hazard. So after several days, we organized a conference call in which about half the group would take part. We made progress and proposed to the whole group that we meet again; a date was set for Sunday, March 28.

For this meeting, Johanna stepped forward to take leadership. With a clear mind, a kind heart, and a calm manner, she circulated an agenda and facilitated the gathering. Dan eloquently articulated the themes on which we already had achieved complete agreement. I reiterated the points that still needed work. Ellen, my assistant, made charts and reflected conclusions. Bit by bit, with that unique brilliance that often flows from "group thinking," questions were answered and language crafted. This time, at the end of the meeting we took extra time for people to search their hearts and minds for tell-tale signs of disquiet. At last, there were none. This time we felt truly done. Michael capped the work by declaring joyfully, "It's not where I wanted to end up, but I'm so happy with how we got here that I can support the agreement whole-heartedly!" The agreement is reproduced in Appendix E.

# 9

# Aftermath

## *Into the Community, Onto the Walls*

NOW THE WORK moved out into the community. Two days after the final meeting, Mauricio posted a notice on his Facebook page:

> This past Sunday, the mediation group met for the 6th session and another 3.5 hours of mediation. We have totaled about 17 hours of meeting time. So after 7 months of mural campaigning and 2 months of mediation we have come to a consensus around the below agreement. It is not perfect, and we are Cautiously Optimistic around the agreement. . . . The current mural will not be restored as is. A new mural/artwork will be created with our participation in the artist(s) selection process and community design process. The vital images of our current mural will be represented in the new mural/artwork as well as Bernal between 1983 and 2009. . . .
>
> Key to the success of the agreement will be your continued participation in the process. It should be much more enjoyable since selecting the artist(s) and participating in the design . . . should be fun since you'll be creating something beautiful and reflective of our historic and cultural contributions. . . .
>
> PS: The billboard comes down April 16th. So take a picture in front of it before it comes down.[1]

1. Save the Bernal Library Mural, Facebook posting, March 31, 2010.

Darcy's group similarly posted a celebratory announcement—and questions poured in: When do we get to say what we think? What will happen next? Who decides?

The next day, Supervisor David Campos arranged to meet again in his City Hall office with the two concerned directors (Luis Herrera of the Library Commission and Luis Cancel of the Arts Commission), plus several of their commissioners. Members of the task force joined me in presenting the consensus statement. The directors and David thrashed out questions of jurisdiction and funding. We talked about how to keep authority in the community and to create a definable body that would accept responsibility. The sense of relief and congratulations was strong as the city officials bent every effort to supporting the next steps.

## Meeting with the Community

Our work was not yet done. We had still to present the agreement to the community and to launch the implementation. We scheduled a community meeting on April 26. David quickly proposed that he host it, an idea I thought intuitively right. This was a moment that called for clear leadership. We decided that David would introduce the gathering and then turn over its facilitation to the mediation group. We agreed it was important for the diversity of the group to be evident, as well as every individual's commitment to the consensus; every member would share the leadership. Over the next several weeks, discussions went forward about forming a task force to implement the agreement. Some people felt it would make the work easier if, at least at the beginning, only people who had taken part in the mediation comprised the task force. Others thought it would be important to begin opening the process to more people who hadn't taken part. In the end, we went with the first idea; for now, it seemed most important that this working group have an existing capability to handle conflict effectively.

We threw membership open to the mediation group. Of the twelve who had participated throughout, eight volunteered: Terry, Darcy, Giulio, Mauricio, Dan, Monique, Brandon, Larry. The other four had competing demands on their time, or felt for one reason or another that it would raise questions of conflict of interest were they to take part. The eight volunteers constituted a great cross-section of the mediation group and of the community.

On the 26th, about seventy-five people met together at the neighborhood center. The mediation group was seated in front of the room. David intended to open the meeting. But in a dilemma familiar to politicians, his schedule ran late. The room filled with chatter and, I sensed, distinct tension. I conferred with the mediation group and suggested I run a community-building exercise while we waited. As it turned out, it was an excellent accident. I had people pair with partners they didn't know and tell the story of their lives—in seven minutes. It's an exercise I learned from Roberto Chené, and it always works splendidly to humanize a convocation and produce a sense of openness in the room. It also constructs an attitude of respectful listening, for that's how I coached people to hear each other.

David arrived while people were still intent on the exercise. Once they were done, he greeted the community and praised the mediation process and participants. I then told the story of what we had done and why, framing it in terms of community relations. Then each member of the mediation group spoke briefly about why they agreed with the proposal we were making. It was both moving and persuasive that such a diverse group of people spoke about their confluence of interests and their excitement at the outcome.

We opened the floor to questions. Most were respectful, but there were some challenges, too. I used the opportunity to extend some skill-building in constructive communication to the wider community. Now and then, I interrupted a speaker, pointed out unnecessary disrespect, and suggested ways to express as much passion without harm to relations. Mauricio especially was the target for some anger. In one exchange with a prominent man in the community, I mediated the dialogue to distinct advantage. Most people have no real wish to injure others, but neither have most people learned alternative ways to speak. I was touched by the receptivity of this man, and of the community in general, to the learning we offered that night. Afterward, I came to understand that the seeming miracle of the mediation group's unanimity stimulated openness in the wider community to the possibility that there really was a better way to conduct disagreement. How much of "bad behavior" stems from a persuasive sense of powerlessness! "We never win," that sentiment that had animated all sides of the controversy in the beginning, was present in the larger community as well. But it was also challenged by the presentation we were offering that night.

We set out a tentative timeline for the next steps and bid each other good night. As far as I could tell, the sounds of leave-taking were appreciative and optimistic.

## Coda

The task force went on to become increasingly skilled at working consensually. The bonds of trust and affection that had grown from the mediation continued to flourish. Darcy and Mauricio were talking almost daily and having an amazingly easy time working through the moments of difference. The group held a couple of events in the neighborhood to raise initial funds and created a plan for proceeding.

But seven months into the work, we were beset by a great tragedy. Some of us knew that Mauricio had been dealing with illness, although he had almost never missed a meeting and certainly showed no diminution of energy or passion. In early September, we got word that he had cancer. Treatment had failed. On October 10, Mauricio Vela died.

His legacy to the community is his dedication to the good fight. As much as I mourned his loss, I was grateful he had been able to transform how he fought before he died, that he left as much love among his erstwhile adversaries as among his comrades. Bringing about change for the better is a reason to live; Mauricio did that, embracing change for himself as well.

At a memorial for Mauricio in the neighborhood center, I read a statement on behalf of the task force:

October 27, 2010

To the Bernal community and Mauricio's family and friends:

We are members of the Bernal Library Artwork Task Force. Throughout 2010, we've worked with Mauricio Vela to resolve a heated controversy about the fate of the mural on the library's walls. Last January, Mauricio joined with a dozen fellow residents of the hill to mediate the controversy, which meant addressing underlying divisions within the neighborhood as well. After three months of intense, exhausting, and exhilarating sessions, the mediation group proposed a solution to the issue: to create new artwork honoring both the potent pre-existing images and also the history and beauty of the building.

Mauricio's role in the process was central. Without him, there might have been no mediation; the issues symbolized by the library walls might have smoldered under the surface, deepening discord and mistrust within the neighborhood. Bernal sees itself as a place that manifests values of equity and respect. Mauricio animated those values by leading a struggle to preserve artwork that, to many on the hill, symbolized social justice. He fanned embers into flame, in the process hurting some people and inspiring others.

Through the mediation process and the subsequent work of the task force, Mauricio built relationships in a different way. Never relinquishing his commitment to the underlying meanings of the mural nor his leadership in the "Save the Mural" movement he organized, he gradually also built new relationships with those whom he initially opposed. Over time, understanding and respect grew on all sides, and in the end we came to collaborate in the good spirit of friendship. Controversy continued, but now it became a constructive act deepening accord rather than division.

We on the task force celebrate Mauricio's ardent participation and mourn our enormous loss.

*The Task Force*: Beth Roy, Brandon Powell, Dan Martinez, Darcy Lee, Giulio Sorro, Larry Cruz, Monique Jaquez, Terry Milne

# Part Two

· · ·

## *Theorizing the Good Fight*

# 10

# Turning Points

HOW DOES CHANGE come about? What are the dynamics operating at those key moments when minds and hearts shift? I want to look more closely at five of those moments during the mediation that seemed to me to be pivotal.

## How a Contest for Rights Transforms into Common Rights

Early in the first session, two comments framed the deeper interests represented in the room. Giulio described his experience as a child when affluent neighbors moved in and scolded the children for playing ball in the street. "I didn't mind their moving in," he told us, "but I did mind their sense of entitlement."

Soon afterward, Brandon interrupted a flow of dialogue with a rhetorical question. "How long," he asked, more in sadness, I thought, than in anger, "do you have to live here before you have standing?"

Each of these expressions might have been innocuous. But in the context of the mediation, they framed the conflict like bookends. Unpacked, they spoke exactly to the history we needed to confront. In one reading, they named the conflict: whose rights were dominant? Did Giulio and his peers have the right to define the culture of the community by virtue of their longevity here? Or did Brandon have rights because he had settled here with his family? What made these statements so informative to me, though, was that underneath the competition for rights I could see a true confluence of interests.

Giulio's statement suggested a rich story of community and culture. It memorialized a time when public streets rang with the play of youngsters growing up in close and friendly proximity. Today, when fears for children's safety keep them trapped indoors, plaguing parents with the endless task of arranging peer social engagements, boys playing noisy ball games in the streets evoke nostalgia for a time gone by. In stable communities where neighbors know each other, where every adult is guardian of every child, both kids and parents enjoy substantial freedom. Having given birth to my son while living in a rural part of India, I deeply believe the natural state of childhood is a pack existence. Where multi-age associations are the norm, children engage each other in ways both beneficial and challenging. Such collectivism sets a cultural standard. In nuclear families kept largely indoors by dangerous times, individual children let off energy in problematic ways. Boredom and isolation spawn belligerence. Conflicts grow over screen time, dinner time, bedtime. Siblings quarrel; parents seek control; children rebel. Individualism and contention are twin cultural artifacts embedded in the structure of nuclear families isolated within four walls.

When Giulio said it was not the arrival of newcomers but rather their entitlement he resented, I heard a thick statement about a lifestyle challenged and with it a set of rights he had deeply assumed before the neighborhood changed. Children had a right to play, a right to the streets, a right to friendship, a right to a far larger degree of autonomy than they today enjoy. His feeling about the mural symbolized that nostalgia. Even more, he resented that the newer neighbors felt entitled to curtail his rights. Although he didn't spell it out, I imagined he attributed their entitlement to class. Did they equate their superior economic status with superior rights to the neighborhood culture they wanted? Neighborhood and community were not identical anymore; Giulio might have been willing to find accommodations that served everyone, but he was not willing to accept an unequal distribution of rights to satisfaction.

When Brandon raised the question of longevity of residence and standing, he too was laying claim to community rights. Brandon was the father of two young boys. An African-American man married to a white woman, he had moved to Bernal and fully engaged in making a rich community for his family. He formed a group called the

Bernal Dads. He co-parented his sons in active partnership with their mother. He welcomed the mediation as a chance to contribute to the construction of the community he wanted for his children, and for himself. By all these many actions, he asserted his right to live in association with others in the ways he valued.

So rights and community were values shared by Brandon and Giulio. Where then did their conflict lie? I doubted that Brandon would scold children for playing in the street, if he thought them safe and respectful. I doubted that Giulio would begrudge Brandon a neighborly welcome. And yet they asserted rights from quite different perspectives. For Giulio, the rights he felt challenged were for cultural primacy, but also for economic security. Brandon's public art aesthetic was probably quite different from Giulio's, and so also was his financial situation. While their perception of conflict had reality to it, their reality actually allowed for a great deal of common ground. Naming both sides of that equation—acknowledging that Brandon, with two professional incomes in his family, was better able to afford the neighborhood than Giulio's family, and at the same time that both families shared an interest in preserving a neighborhood where community thrived—was an essential framing for mediation. It was also noteworthy that both men manifested new realities of multiracial identity. Giulio was the product of a marriage between parents of two races, and so also were Brandon's children.

### How Perceptions of Powerlessness
### Become Experiences of Acting Powerfully

When I spoke with members of the mediation after the first session and heard from each of them the same statement of powerlessness, I was surprised. Every individual present at that table had spoken eloquently. Each of them had very ably begun to form relationships with others. Every position expressed had credibility and each was well argued.

Why then was there this prevalent belief on all sides that "we never win"?

If Giulio and Brandon's statements articulated basic interests in establishing *rights*, this statement spoke to people's assessment of their *power* to assert their rights. Mauricio expressed angry pessimism in the context of other battles lost. Most recently, he referenced the pre-school controversy. Although the pre-school continued to exist, it had lost the library space. Some people in the community saw the new location as preferable in a number of ways. It put the children in contact with older kids in the elementary school where it was now housed. The library basement had been damp and dark; some people insisted it was infested with vermin. The new site was maintained by the school district, which was debatably an advantage.

But clearly for Mauricio, beyond the advantages and disadvantages of each site, the battle lost had been about the will of the community. His community, that is, as he defined it. And that was a population that was in fact losing ground. Many people had moved away from Bernal as property values skyrocketed. More upscale stores and restaurants redefined the cost and culture of Cortland Avenue. Renters were priced out of the market, and longtime home owners cashed out equity to use for retirement.

For Mauricio and many of his followers, therefore, the mural had high symbolic value. He did not truly believe that property values would stabilize or decline if the mural were to be saved. He fought instead for a spirit of survival. But even as he fought, that spirit was bedeviled by the realities of gentrification, a seemingly unstoppable force.

On the other side of the conflict, people expressed parallel expectations of powerlessness. There was a generalized sense that a political fix was in. Unwilling to be seen as abandoning their more disadvantaged constituents—so went this story line—the mayor and commissions would not dare antagonize Mauricio and his troops. There were racial overtones to the analysis: both commission directors were Latino, as was the Bernal supervisor. David Campos was widely acknowledged to be a leader of the progressive forces in the city; surely he would side with Mauricio. The neighborhood center also had political clout; from the outside, it seemed a seamless part of Mauricio's campaign.

In actuality, all those segments of city life represented far more nuanced interests and values. The neighborhood center was dealing with internal struggles occasioned in large part by economic hard times and a dramatic loss of city funding for their programs. David, as we learned in the course of the mediation, was a far broader and deeper thinker than his constituents might have thought him to be, based on the sound bites that constitute political campaigns. Luis Herrera, the City Librarian, believed profoundly in the benefits of community autonomy; he strongly supported whatever solution arose from Bernal itself.

The perception of powerlessness on both sides was a profound assumption based, I believe, in a widespread alienation from American public life. So many people experience themselves as helpless in the face of national forces far beyond their control. Economics, street violence, foreign wars, legislative stalemates affect the daily lives of individuals without their consent. That sense of powerlessness pervades even situations in which people can and do take powerful action. A concept I find invaluable is internalized oppression. We do in fact suffer oppression. Witness the real difficulty of having political impact. Witness the helplessness with which people close to retirement age watched their funding vanish in 2008. Witness a thousand other events of life—downsizing corporations, inaccessible healthcare, discrimination against gay couples, police violence toward black and Latino men, not to mention real economic discrimination, and on and on. At the same time, we generalize from those experiences and stories to form a belief that we are more powerless than we in fact are.

When the need to act in the public domain becomes dire enough—and many people saw the library mural to be one such place—the contradiction between behavior and internalized oppression becomes severe. We act, but how effectively? Feeling powerless at the same time that we speak out, we may well act badly. The contradiction is painful, and so we inflict pain on others. We call the mural ugly; we call our adversaries racists. The weapons of the weak are many and complex; they may be creative, but they are also often counterproductive.

In the mediation, people were able to experience the powers they in fact possessed: to speak honestly, to move and influence others, to think together creatively, and to elicit support from public sources they had seen as unfeeling and unhelpful. One piece of getting there was to name the contradiction and to call forth faith that we as a group could get beyond it. I did that when I challenged people to look beneath the words, "We never win," and to find a way to reveal that statement as an untrue and counterproductive prediction.

## How Genuine Emotion Opens Up Insight

One of the extraordinary powers the mediatees demonstrated was the ability to speak honestly about what they felt. Clearing the air was an essential part of the mediation process. Not only did people need to heal past injuries, but they also needed to know that they could continue to build interpersonal alliances as the mediation proceeded, even when someone did something that offended them. To speak openly about these moments and to experience the relief of being fully heard was to experience the power of both voice and heart. And that happened again and again. At every meeting, people worked through crossed transactions, large and small. The distinction made no difference; if it pinched, it mattered. To re-experience these successes time after time was to defeat pessimism when it came to the negotiation itself. Not only did we practice acting powerfully, but we built deeper and deeper insight into each other's feelings and lives. Building relationships of caring in this way carried the negotiation forward.

One pivotal moment was, of course, the exchange between Dan and Darcy. I've already commented on why that moment was so important. Here, I want to elaborate on why it was so transformative.

The day after that meeting, I called Dan to see if he needed any support. I was concerned that he had been so revealing and worried that he might feel vulnerable in some way. On the contrary, he told me he felt permanently changed. "Even while I was saying that I'd always been a stereotype and always would be," he said, "I was making a decision that I would never be a stereotype again." That was a change, he knew, not in how others might see him—assumptions based on ethnic stereotypes die hard—but it was a profound change in him. From that moment, he determined that he would believe within himself in his dignity and in his right to be seen as a dimensional person.

As our work went forward, he demonstrated that self-regard again and again. Our theory of internalized oppression sees it operating through false ideas. Enormously persuasive, often urging us to believe ourselves more powerless than we are, these ideas are learned, and they can be unlearned. Dan had just demonstrated exactly that process.

Meanwhile, Darcy's learning about the culture she had demeaned was greatly expanded. The artwork on the library was so clearly not just images painted on a wall. It was an expression of values and relationships about which she could know nothing unless others, in this case Dan, told her. The car depicted in the mural was a counter-stereotype. A circle of young Bernal men of Latino heritage shared a passion for vintage cars. These were not lowriders; they had not been adapted in the stylized way stereotypically associated with young Latino men. Instead, they were cars lovingly restored to their historical forms. A great deal of artistry, scholarship, and mechanical skill went into the hobby, and it was an undertaking especially prized by certain young men who had grown up on the hill.

There was no way Darcy might have known any of this if Dan hadn't explained it. There was no way Dan would have explained it if he had heard Darcy's comment as a slur and gone away mad. Because enough air had been cleared and enough camaraderie established by that moment, Dan took the risk to speak honestly and emotionally in the group. By doing that, by expressing his pain, he changed not only Darcy's perceptions but also the belief in the group in general that change could happen, that *they* could bring about change together. Good feeling was advanced, but even more importantly, internalized oppression was dispelled for everyone, not only Dan.

### How Leadership Emerges and Is Shared

It was a breathtaking moment when, at the end of the second session, Larry proposed a solution to the mural issue. As the formal leader of the discussion, I had not identified the moment as a time to come to a conclusion. But sensing the unity built so strongly in the room by the stories we had heard and the emotions we had shared, Larry leapt ahead to focus that good feeling on a resolution. He led the majority to agreement, but there was not yet consensus in the group. In fact, his exuberant proposal stimulated push-back from Mauricio. He rose as if to leave. He objected to further meetings at Larry's house. He expressed anger at Larry for advocating the removal of the mural from the Cortland façade.

Even though the moment of leadership was premature, in the sense that the group was not there yet, it was enormously productive, for several reasons. It symbolized the extent to which power was moving from me as leader to the members of the group. They were taking possession of the process, not in opposition to me but in partnership. Also, a concrete proposal focused the discussion to come. It clarified where strongly-held opinions remained and where dissension still needed to be worked through.

There were many other moments when similar acts of leadership were contributed by other people. Johanna assumed the facilitation of a later meeting. Monique frequently spoke up decisively when others hesitated to state their opinions forcefully. Michael intervened at moments of impasse with imaginative ideas from far outside the box. Amy carried news of the process to the outside world in her communications to her circle, and Darcy similarly acted as a responsible reporter using Facebook. Brandon always named that which was unspoken in the room, fearlessly and with heart.

Each time someone came forward to initiate movement in the dialogue, embers of hope were fanned into life. In the dynamics of groups, courage and initiative continually inspire a sense of possibility where silence douses the fire.

### How a Wider Lens of Understanding Leads to More Options

Although there were many other critical points on the path toward consensus, I want to end this discussion by writing a bit more about the importance of putting the dispute in a larger context. Blame is perhaps one of the most universal qualities of conflict. We look for someone who is at fault. The dispute would not have escalated had Mauricio not called people racist. The Save the Mural forces would not have become so ardent had Darcy not described the mural as ugly in her petition.

For some, the fault lay with the city leadership. Not knowing which commission was in charge meant a vacuum of decision-making power; dissension flows swiftly into a vacuum. Why hadn't the city librarian just made a decision and stuck with it? Why had the commissioners not heeded the reasonable voices of those arguing for clean walls?

At the same time, there were contesting stories about the issue circulating in the community. The problem was gentrification—all those selfish, rich, young dot-commers moving in to destroy the neighborhood. The problem was Latino retrogrades—people who defined themselves as oppressed and claimed special rights as a result. Each of these stories not only pointed fingers somewhere, but they also contributed mightily to a sense of powerlessness. Nobody was going to stop people moving in from Silicon Valley. Nobody was going to convince fourth-generation Latino neighbors that they should passively accept displacement from their family homes. What we might be able to change when unified we could only bemoan helplessly divided.

When we laid out the ever-expanding contexts for conflict, we were also able to identify the places where we could and could not make a difference. We were not going to solve the problems of an economy that was exploding vast differences in wealth under the influence of globalization, runaway financial markets, and the technology revolution. But we could build a community of caring, where people come together to help neighbors stay in their homes. We were not going to stop the flow of high-tech businesses to San Francisco at the cost of more blue-collar jobs. But we could humanize relations in the neighborhood by understanding the costs and benefits of changes and ensuring that everyone shared in the benefits and worked to ameliorate the costs. And we could do those things through a process of double vision: one eye on the immediate dispute, the library artwork; the other eye on the larger causes of community distress.

Sarah Cobb, a scholar of conflict, calls moments of potential change in mediation liminal moments (Cobb 2001). To use a metaphor from physics, they are the energetic spaces when the pendulum gains the potential to swing the other way. They are pregnant spaces from which many different consequences can flow. The events I've discussed here constituted some of those moments. As a mediator, I see my job as helping people construct these spaces, naming the moments when they come, and supporting people to use them to good purpose.

Through all these moments, changes were taking place in dealing with the immediate conflict, and also on very personal levels, as both identities and feelings of possibility expanded.

# 11

# Dynamics of Mediating
# Identity-Based Conflict

THE NARRATIVE of the Bernal mediation is descriptive on the level of interaction. As people spoke honestly and emotionally about their lives, other people's understanding grew, and with understanding came compassion. These moments of change were embedded in structures, however, that continued to exist. I think of "structures" as frameworks that reside both externally in the real world outside the rooms where we worked, and also internally, in the hearts and minds of each individual involved. Clearly, those two realms are not distinct. What Mauricio or Brandon or Darcy or Monique brought into the room— their feelings and thoughts, their beliefs and interests—had all grown over years of experience in interaction with their families, communities, schools, workplaces, and so on. At the same time, what was happening among us as we grappled with the relationships and problems of the moment changed us all, and in turn impacted the community we shared.

Three concepts that frame understandings of conflict were very apparent in the Bernal experience: identity, interests, and power. Too often we regard identity as impenetrable and static, as if by identifying a given individual as "Latino" we can know for certain what that person thinks and feels about an issue. Mauricio identified as Latino and he championed the cause of preserving the mural as a symbol of the Latino community on the hill. Monique also identified as Latina. In addition, she identified as a third-generation Bernal dweller. In her twenties, after having moved away in her young adulthood, she returned to the home in which she'd started in order to care for her aging grandparents. When she came to formulate her position about the library mural, her Latina heritage was only one of several identities that shaped her view. She was young; her friendship circle included gay people, artists of a variety of heritages, newcomers to the neighborhood, and so on. She argued for art that better represented the community as she knew it—quite a different community from the one Mauricio defined.

Mauricio's engagement was motivated by his interest in mobilizing and representing those people of color whom he saw to be disadvantageously challenged by gentrification. Monique's engagement was motivated by her commitment to Bernal's history, not as a representation only of the past, but also of the present community. After working on the project for over a year, the task force reviewed each member's will to continue. Monique spoke eloquently of how much her grandparents had given to Bernal and her dedication to continuing that tradition. For Mauricio, contributing meant artistic preservation; for Monique, it meant artistic change. Mauricio's initial position was to save the mural; Monique's was to create new art. Mauricio's underlying interest was to create an empowered constituency; Monique's was to honor and extend her forebears' values of community engagement.

Breaking down assumptions about identity allows for a fine-tuned articulation of interests, and, as Fisher and Ury have theorized in *Getting to Yes* (1981), interests are amenable to elaboration in ways that abet the construction of common ground.

As I write, California has recently become a minority–majority state. That is, no single racial or ethnic group any longer forms a majority of the population. In the United States as a whole, people of European heritage are still a majority, but by a margin that is diminishing year by year. In the presidential election of 2012, voting patterns were significantly altered as Latino citizens joined African-Americans, LGBT people, voters of Asian origins, and young voters to give President Obama a decisive victory. The gender gap, long suggesting a split between Democratic-leaning women and Republican-leaning men, widened across all lines of identity. For many people, what it means to be American and the national identity have forever changed, a fact some celebrate, others mourn. Moreover, identities that were once hidden are increasingly becoming evident: gay and lesbian, gender challenging, invisibly disabled, all once protectively hidden in the private domain have now become public.

Each of these transformations suggests ways that identity and power are linked. Each has resulted from political actions that have served dramatically to impact cultural values and assumptions. On the one hand, identity is often used to inspire a political constituency to act against oppression, material or symbolic, as Mauricio did. Evocations of shared identity can mobilize people for united political action despite rather disparate interests. The news is full of stories about "identity-based conflicts" around the world, most of them assumed to be "age-old and intractable." In reality, we need to ask what caused given groups with like identities to act when and how they do, and why they have united around an identity rather than a cause, if in fact they have.

Identity can also be the concept around which people assert claims to privilege. Some time ago, I studied contemporary dynamics of racism by interviewing white people who had been students at a major southern high school at the time it was desegregated some forty years earlier. They agreed to talk with me because I resembled them. I, too, had attended a segregated high school, graduating the year before all hell had broken loose in their school. "We believe you can tell our story," they said, having made a shared decision to talk with me. Again and again, they told me that their passivity in the face of violent resistance to school integration was simply an expression of a way of life they had always known. "Belonging" was a central concept to them. One of the black students newly enrolled in "their" school was a young woman of presence and pride. One white student told me, "We didn't object to them coming to our school, but she walked the halls as if she belonged there." Here, identity, power, and privilege intersected. The African-American youngster could attend the white school—she had that power, thanks to the Supreme Court's desegregation decision—but claiming the privilege of belonging betrayed the racial hierarchy and was unacceptable (Roy 1999, 171–96).

Somewhere near the core of all political action are dynamics of power. Indeed, we can expand that statement to say that all conflict involves power contestation on some level. I've offered a multi-dimensional way of thinking about power; now I want to consider the ways that identity intersects power.

First and most obviously, in the United States and much of the rest of the world, power is unequally distributed among groups of varied identities. Labels of majority and minority often mask realities of domination. Second, when more direct means are lacking for people to act on their most urgent interests, often they unite around identities, typically ethnically based. This pull toward ethnicity is understandable in light of common assumptions, some of which I've already referenced: that people of like identity will share worldviews, cultures, and therefore interests, as well. There are many examples, however, of ethnically-based mobilizations that encompass multiple internal conflicts. Often, lines of friction fall along accustomed differences of class, gender, generation, location, and so on. But people gravitate toward forming the most effective collaborative available when problems press; when more direct forms of action based in shared interests are not available, identity may seem to offer the next best hope of amassing enough power to win demands.

In Bernal, an interest in providing equal access to resources, including residence in the neighborhood, was much more widespread than any ethnic identity suggested. In fact, Mauricio was persuaded to join the mediation by his recognition that the lines along which he was organizing may have been interfering with the formation of alliances across ethnic lines in this controversy as well as future battles. By campaigning stridently, as he did, he may have strengthened his position around the mural, but was he weakening his potential effectiveness to mobilize a wider constituency around issues like affordable housing, immigrant rights, and availability of educational resources? In reality, these issues more closely reflected Mauricio's deepest interests than did the mural. Not that the mural itself, as symbol and as organizing

issue, wasn't important, but Mauricio's core values were for social justice, a goal attained not by murals but by access to resources.

So at the same time that identity maps lines of social inequality,
it also can be used as a rallying point for challenging injustice. It can
reflect differences of privilege and oppression, and also be a source of
power. Beyond the uses of identity for political mobilization, its power
also lies in group loyalty and cultural pride. In which exact "culture"
a given individual takes pride may vary widely, however, as demonstrated by differences in the meanings attached to the Bernal mural by
Mauricio and Monique.

All of us entertain not one but a multiplicity of identities, for we all
occupy a multiplicity of worlds. In *Some Trouble with Cows*, I explored
in some detail why a group of farmers in South Asia mobilized as Hin-
dus and Muslims rather than as peasants at a given moment of historic
change in their area (Roy 1994). Identity is fluid and sensitive to conditions. Which of our many identities rises to the fore in a given moment
is often a product of our relationship to power. When I stand in front
of a class I'm teaching, my identity as professorial elder is strong. But
when I walk down a dark and deserted street at night, my identity as
frail older woman is very much to the fore. Mostly, I have only background consciousness of the fact that my heritage is Jewish. But on
occasion I'm in a room where someone says something that strikes me
as anti-Semitic, and then I look around for the support of assessing
who else is Jewish. Recently, the government of Israel announced a
policy that would inevitably weaken the negotiating position of Pales-
tinians in their ongoing negotiations. I felt very Jewish suddenly, and
very disapproving. I also felt compelled to question my responsibility
as a Jew. The identity attributed to me most often is that of a straight
woman; however, my partner of many years is a woman and I identify
as a lesbian, especially when there is anti-gay sentiment in the room
and I want to "come out" in order to lend support.

▪     ▪     ▪

Much more could be written about identity, interests, and power. I've
touched on these topics because they were central to the Bernal mediation and because I believe these themes to be woven through most if

not all conflicts. However close to the surface or unarticulated, however obvious or subtle, identity is the place from which we venture forth to fight, the home we protect. To understand that home can be redefined in the cause of naming and negotiating interests gives us crucial power to use conflict as transformation at the deepest levels.

# Part Three

. . .

## *Pragmatics and Reflections*

# 12

# Summarizing the Model

IT IS NOT ACCIDENTAL that my story of the Bernal mediation ends with a celebration of positive changes in personal relationships. The work I do arose from a particular blending of community and individual transformation. Called radical psychiatry or radical therapy, its premise is to place individual behaviors and feelings in a social context (Roy 2007; Steiner 1981). In this chapter, I outline the approach I generally use, revisiting the Bernal mediation to illustrate both its features and the need for flexibility when applying any "model" to real life. Much of the theory I'm going to recount here is not original with me; my work is thoroughly steeped in a tradition and a philosophy I share with my colleagues. You'll find that much of what I present here repeats my earlier narrative but from a more theoretical perspective.

Both theory and practice are grounded in two foundational principles:

- *People are good.* We do the best we can given the conditions we experience, too many of which are oppressive. In practice, this assumption means trusting the honest intentions of people with whom we work. With some guidance, the expectation is that participants are not acting strategically but are seeking help to present their stories and interests openly and genuinely.

- *People are sane.* If we assume that what people feel and say makes sense, then we search for meaning in what we might instead dismiss with a diagnosis. Most often, having dignified the communication and helped people to clarify its expression, we do in fact find sense.

## The Context: Exploring the Terrain
## and Preparing the Fundamentals

These two premises mobilize a series of questions and actions. If good people are behaving badly, then my first act is to listen to the unguarded stories they tell in the privacy of conversation with me. Sometimes, I don't have an opportunity to talk with everyone who will subsequently take part in the mediation, although the ideal is to do just that. I do, however, ask each person I speak with to tell me a bit about what's going on. Knowing that I'm hearing about the conflict from one perspective only, these conversations nonetheless tell me a great deal, as long as I can hold in abeyance my internal conclusions. Often, the stories I hear are filled with pain. They are tales of wrongs and losses suffered, emotional cries that evoke compassion. But if they also pull on a wish to "fix it," to intervene as advocate for the person harmed based on only that one perspective, then mediating becomes problematic. If I can maintain that degree of distance that allows me to hear all other stories with equivalent compassion, then I'm gathering helpful information rather than prejudging the situation. It's often helpful to hear accounts from people not directly involved in the conflict. This "gossip"—again, held judiciously—can also be informative.

### The Setup: Composition and Design

One use of these pre-stories is figuring out who should be present in the intervention work itself. The Bernal case involved a very high degree of interviewing and exploring before I designed the intervention and selected the participants. In that case, I was looking for people who could speak both in their own personae and who also could reflect and influence a wider constituency's views. Most mediations don't contain this particular, political element, although I would say that any conflict resolution impacts a wider circle of people and dynamics than present in the room, simply because none of us exists in isolation. When we change, so do others with whom we are connected. In family mediations and organizational interventions, the need to think "outside the box" about who should take part is very real. In both these settings, conflict often is defined as a personality clash between two people, just as Mauricio Vela, the community activist, and Darcy Lee, the business leader, two very public and emotionally articulate people, seemed to propel the Bernal conflict. A little digging beneath the surface almost always reveals that the most apparent disputes have deeper roots in family and organizational dynamics. Should the two sisters who can't sit across from each other at the Thanksgiving table come alone? Or is a third, well-loved sister, chosen by the parents to be executor of their wills, also central to the dynamic? At what point do the parents need to be involved? Similarly, constructing organizational conflict interventions almost always involves pushing for wider group involvement.

The next question is time. It is a common error to negotiate too little time to do a thorough job. So many mediators today work in agency or court settings where they are under pressure to work quickly and end with settlements. The work is seriously handicapped by timelines that do not allow for full expression and comprehensive understanding of what's at issue. As an independent mediator, I have the great luxury of scheduling ample time: three to four hours for a two-person session, a full day for a group of ten or more. Of course, time and money intersect, so I also charge on a sliding scale intended to make my work accessible to as many people as possible.

By this time, I usually have a fair sense of cultural and identity dimensions of the conflict. Do I need to partner with someone who can grasp and work with those elements better than I can? This, too, often becomes a question of money. In the old days of radical therapy, we never mediated solo. Once we were earning our livings doing the work, two mediators in most cases became too expensive for many clients, so we reluctantly gave it up. Partnering with another accomplished mediator is a treat; it serves well both for the interveners and for the participants. Conflicts are complex creatures; the more hands working to tame them the better. What is always a luxury becomes a necessity when the composition of the group or the nature of the dispute is beyond my cultural reach. I may be well prepared to understand common dynamics of "-isms"; I've devoted a great deal of my professional career and my personal life to anti-oppression work—enough to know that there are many things I cannot know. I may be as open as humanly possible to learning about those things, but in the intense course of conflict transformation, mediatees should not have to be responsible for educating the mediator. So, partnering is an act of recognition and respect. I began working with Cynthia Luna from the beginning of the Bernal mediation, because her background as an immigrant from Mexico (combined with her enormous talent and skill!) gave her the capacity for insight I did not have. She was also able to help bridge trust on the part of participants, should that become needed. When co-mediating really matters, it is important enough that rather than do without it, I remain open to adjusting fees to make it affordable.

As these pre-mediation conversations go on and the composition of the work takes shape, I start preparing people for coming together to do the work. Earlier, I outlined the steps we use in a typical mediation:

- Homework
- Goals
- Exchange of feelings
- Analysis
- Negotiation of changes
- Plan for implementation
- "Strokes"

Starting with the instruction to prepare written notes for sessions, each step reflects my trust that people bring the greatest degree of honesty, or goodness, to the work that they can. In other words, I take it on faith that what they describe as their experiences makes sense when viewed from within a particular standpoint. Writing lists of feelings linked to perceived events utilizes the relationship between mind and feeling to help make sense of emotion. Writing moves consciousness from a psychic location that is visceral to one that is mindful. Buddhists speak of a higher "I"; a client of mine uses the colorful phrase "helicoptering over." We all engage this process from time to time. In the passion of a moment, all we can do is scream and cry. But later we put words to what we felt, articulating a story that encompasses both what the emotions were and how they came to be. To take pen in hand—or more commonly these days, keyboard—is to engage language in the service of emotion, and the language we suggest is intended to bypass judgment in favor of accuracy. So people come to mediation having already done a good deal of the work, because the shift from raw emotion to thoughtful words, descriptive of perceived behaviors and experienced emotions, enables both communicative exchange and instrumental change.

A central element in mediation is actually teaching. I use a variety of concepts in the course of the work. One model that describes the process of linking emotion and thoughtful expression visualizes three forms of internal process: Parent, Adult, Child (Steiner 2009; Wyckoff 1980). The Child is feeling, creativity, intuition, sexuality—all somatic manifestations of self. The Adult is thinking, analysis, learned skills like language, and so on. Ideally, Child and Adult work together: Child informs Adult; Adult communicates Child in ways that produce effective action in the world. Parent, however, may interfere. In the more political conception of radical therapy, Parent is the repository of social values. It consists of ideas learned through social interaction, both firsthand within the family and immediate environment, and culturally through media and community mores. We define two versions of Parent, one positive or nurturing, the other disempowering, a manifestation of internalized oppression. This latter form often interferes with an individual's capacity to engage in conflict constructively, because manifest oppression is internalized as the denial of the right to feel what one feels, to express what one wants, and so on.

The notes I ask people to write in advance are strictly for their own use. I ask them not to consult with the people with whom they are mediating (although consultation with others who are not involved is often very helpful). The guidelines I send for doing the homework vary from situation to situation, but in general they cover the following territory:

- What are your goals for the mediation?
- List your "Held Feelings"—events that have caused you distress and what you felt. (I provide the formula for framing these statements and some examples.)
- What changes would you ideally like to have happen?

For the Bernal mediation, in the context of neighborhood relations, we asked questions relevant to the issue at hand. We also asked participants to think about positive responses to others, a means to challenge some of the alienation that we knew to exist. When mediating more intimate folks—couples or family members or friends—I rarely ask for this fourth list, because people in close personal relationships may take the instruction to "think positively" as an injunction against giving voice to the hard feelings, precisely those that need to be fully aired if conflict is to lead to progressive change. Love flows after distressed feelings have been expressed, understood, and transformed into positive change.

Through the use of homework, mediatees enter the process having had an opportunity to sort and articulate their experience, and that activity may also have helped to dignify their feelings. I have occasionally found myself out of a job when clients canceled a mediation after having made their notes and moved right along to a satisfying dialogue with each other. To me, that constitutes success.

**The Beginning: Goals, Roles, and Power Relations**

Once people do appear for the session, the process builds on their notes. Radical therapy jargon for the setting of goals is "making a contract." Often, innovation prompts a search for particular vocabularies in which to name new concepts. New jargon is created, borrowed, problematically, from very different enterprises, and sometimes it misleads as much as it elucidates. The language of "transactions," "clients," "contracts," and so on derives from business and legal dealings, not exactly the cultural framework for work seated in contexts of heart and politics. "Contract" is in fact a misnomer—it is not a binding agreement—but it contains a kernel of truth. In stating goals we are negotiating a particular relationship. The mediatees are saying, "Here's what we want your help with." And I, as the mediator, am responding honestly with an assurance that I believe I can provide that help.

But can I? Firming up the goals for a mediation is another exercise in listening. There are several things to listen for: Am I clear about what each person wants? Sometimes it is necessary to ask some questions, to make sure that what the person is asking to do is behavioral and can be accomplished in the context of the session. In most interpersonal mediations, the crafting of goals can be done in the room; it forms a good introduction to the work to come. But organizational mediations require more work in advance, and so I carry on fairly elaborate conversations with as many people as I can, both participants and on-lookers, exploring layered expectations and hopes. In the Bernal mediation, this process was woven into the initial interviews I conducted as I selected participants. I was forthright in discussing with people what I believed could and could not be accomplished. From the very beginning I wanted to make sure the mediation's sponsor, Supervisor David Campos, was clear about my own sense of limitations, and later the conversations I had with Mauricio Vela further explored possible goals at the same time that we explored benefits and costs to him and to his constituents.

Some of the questions I keep in mind are: Do I hear contradictions between or among the various goals that suggest there can be no truly collaborative solution? The classic example of this problem is the couple, one of whom wants a baby and one of whom does not. I can't mediate a solution to that difference in interests that will come close to taking care of both parties. I might offer to help with a conversation about what that means for their relationship, what some alternatives might be, and so on. But from the start, I will not hold out hope that there can be a collaborative agreement achieved at the end. Similarly, I carefully framed the Bernal mediation in terms of community relations, not murals and libraries. That it progressed into a negotiated solution was a product of the participants, not of my promise, implied or explicit.

Finally, more subtly, does my intuition tell me that the articulated goal gives me permission to intervene in the ways I believe will be most helpful? An example of this problem is a supervisor who wants good relations with her employees, but already in laying out her goals has expressed hurtful judgments a number of times. In that case, I might suggest a further goal: to get some constructive feedback about her manner of giving criticism. This situation is a clear opportunity to negotiate my power as a mediator to actually help the participants to achieve their goals. If anybody is closed either to certain kinds of suggestions or particular changes, then my power to intervene is limited. I prefer to speak that limitation at the beginning rather than encountering it at an unsatisfactory end. Once voiced, limitations have a way of being overcome. People come to mediation only after struggle has failed. They want help, and mostly they are open to becoming aware of their own roles in the conflict. Inviting a participant to accept critical feedback constructs a power relationship that is wholly in the interest of everyone being mediated. It is assuming the role of guide, leader, advocate, counselor, all rolled into one.

As I explored possibilities for the Bernal mediation, my early conversations with Mauricio demonstrate this process well: together, we identified the cost to him of his way of engaging in conflict. Once he had expressed how hurtful it was to know that his adversaries were so angry at him, and once I had held out a vision of another way for conflict to be handled, he was very open to my critical reflections on his choice of language and strategy for mobilizing protest. I acted in this case as teacher, nurturer, critic, and above all, advocate for his protection as well as the well-being of the community.

## Storytelling: Emotion and Meaning

Once the goals are clearly stated and the relevant roles accorded to the mediator, the next stage is often the longest and the most intense: clearing the air. I structure this conversation, intervening frequently for the sake both of fruitful dialogue and teaching. There may be good reason behind each person's position in any conflict, but those reasons may be obscured by the way people are communicating.

Cultural norms for expressing emotionally charged matters tend to be judgmental, argumentative, and escalatory. Conflicts therefore often become more and more polarized the more people try to press their point. The more polarized they become, the more heated are emotions and the more hurtful their expression. What lies at the root of conflict becomes obscured, covered in layers of hurt, anger, and fear.

In the storytelling part of mediation, the mediator therefore has three goals:

1) To guide and structure an exchange of feelings in a new way, avoiding judgment and naming emotion with accuracy

2) To teach skills that can be used in daily life, making intervention a rare necessity

3) To seek insight into the most central differences animating the conflict by paying close attention to the content of the emotional exchange

The most familiar way to tell a story is structured by time and purpose. We begin at the beginning and end with our point. Some details we choose to include, others to omit, choices strategized with an argumentative goal in mind. The listener must either interrupt—interruption being a no-no in most conflict resolution modalities—or must bide her time for a long time, accumulating her own counter-points and building up more and more argumentative steam.

To structure dialogue through the use of "I-statements" produces several results. First, it privileges the subjective, not abstractly over other forms of reality, but as an essential starting place. The lens is emotional, although the form I use, naming a perceived action and linking it with an experienced feeling, also provides a window into perceptual differences that is helpful. These statements are brief and spare; the form does not encourage poetic elaboration, however strong the temptation, because embedded in lyricism too often is judgment. Metaphoric speech may feel satisfying, but it is inexact; it compares one precise thing to another expressive one at the cost of accuracy. My work as a mediator has turned me into a word-hound. By paying close attention to how disrespect is communicated in common speech, I've come to appreciate how much language both is shaped by cultures of emotion, and in turn constrains and directs emotionality. English works against nonjudgmental expression of feeling, just as northern European cultures tend to be unfriendly to emotional expressiveness. Long words tend to be more problematic than short ones. I sometimes shock my clients by telling them that anything longer than two syllables is likely to be a judgment, not a feeling. "Disappointed," for instance, judges from a place of assumed superiority. It conveys the idea that you've fallen short of my standards. If you think that's true, you might feel sad, angry, worried—a lot of different emotions, but "disappointed" expresses none of them. Similarly, "frustrated" is what I call an umbrella word; under it shelter feelings of powerlessness (one of the few three-syllable words that does seem close enough to emotional experience to let stand), fear, or anger. In mediation, as people take turns speaking what they observed and felt, one statement at a time, the listener is enjoined to simply listen—another important skill most of us need to learn!—hearing the words not as right or wrong but as windows into the consciousness of the other. Words that convey judgments, however, invite defensive argument. Speaker and listener need to partner to bring about constructive communication.

Occasionally, people argue with the idea that judgment is not helpful. "But it's what I feel!" they'll claim. I make the sharpest distinctions possible between three modes of thinking and expression: judgment, opinion, feeling. Emotion quite literally resides in the body. It is not accidental that the Greeks connected particular emotions with organs: heart with love, lungs with powerlessness ("no breathing room"), liver with anger, spleen with envy. The Hindu understanding of chakras and Chinese energy systems are both emotionally linked. In English, we speak of emotions as "feelings," the same word we use for physical sensation.

Judgment, I strongly believe, often arises when emotions go unexpressed. "Stamps," feelings unexpressed that don't go away but are saved up for an uproar, are usually expressed as judgment. If you remember the model I presented earlier of Parent, Adult, and Child, judgment is a manifestation of negative Parent. It is characterized by generalization, a statement that is clearly not true some part of the time (e.g., saying "You are lazy!" to a teenager who won't take out the garbage but who will spend hours and hours programming a computer). Judgment contains morality ("you are bad because you won't take out the garbage"), which can be argued from the point of view of a different value system. It contains both injunctions ("you should take out the garbage") and attributions ("you are bad and lazy if you don't"). Understandably, most people on the receiving end of statements like these will resist, either fighting back or going tactically passive, saving the rebellion for later.

The third category I define is opinion. An adult might say, "I think taking out the garbage may be a good chore for you to take on, because you only have to do it a couple of times a week, and because it helps me more than other things, given my bad back." There is no judgment in that statement. The teenager could voice a different opinion, or a feeling ("I hate the smell of garbage. How about if I do this, that, and the other thing instead, and maybe we could hire the kids next door to take out the garbage?"). Statements from the Adult may link up with feelings ("I've felt angry when I've had to take out the garbage and want to propose that you do it in exchange for sweeping the kitchen floor"), but they do not contain any judgment.

For purposes of conflict resolution, clean communication is of paramount importance. Not only does it allow for emotions to clarify, but it also provides crucial information about the central issues involved. Perhaps most important, it gives people an experience of talking in a way that is respectful yet honest, thorough yet spare. Once having experienced this kind of communication, they take away tools with which to work through problems that arise thereafter.

The statement of feelings in the "I-statement" (or "stamps" or "held feelings"—jargon adheres to "professional" practices like barnacles), familiar to so many schools of conflict resolution, is accompanied in radical therapy practice by the very powerful concept for revealing and accounting for assumptions, intuitions, fears, and other forms of mind reading. We call it *paranoia*,[1] provocatively claiming that it is not pathology but heightened awareness. We all do it; we fill in meaning where it is not explicitly available. We create stories to account for perceptions. If people are not crazy or lying, then the stories they create are based in something real. However, the more we are unable to get validation for our perceptions, the more distorted the stories may become. Checking out *paranoias* is therefore an important act of reconstructing realities that may have become obscured and inflammatory in the course of conflict.

If we commonly read between the lines, we do so all the more intensively in the midst of conflict. Insecurity breeds *paranoia*, rightfully so, since the more vulnerable we are the more we need to assess dangers both overt and covert. We become more and more highly attuned to that which is not spoken, noting body language, silence, the choice of particular words, and making meaning from those signals in a self-protective way. The longer conflict proceeds without direct dialogue about these creative impositions on communication, the more distorted they are likely to become. To articulate them is therefore an extraordinarily helpful act, provided that the listener responds with truth. It is only after we have had our perceptions accounted for that we can hear corrections to the construct we've made. It is very common for people on the receiving end of *paranoias* to try to deny them:

> "I think you don't like me because you didn't say hello when we ran into each other three months ago."

---

1. In clinical practice, paranoia is considered to be a manifestation of mental illness. Seen as psychotic fantasy, any reality that paranoid thoughts might have are dismissed. Popular usage of the word accepts this disregard and steers awareness away from what truth might be contained in a story defined as "paranoid." Radical therapy turns this interpretation on its head, asserting that every perception of another's reality contains some truth. Clinical and popular notions of paranoia stop inquiry; the radical therapy understanding of *paranoia*—which is italicized in the present volume to distinguish it from the clinical and popular usage described above—demands investigation, often leading to new understandings and possibilities for resolving conflict. See also the related discussion in chap. 4.

"No, no, I don't dislike you! I think very highly of you."

"I don't believe you. If you like me, why would you be so cold?"

And silently, "If you liked me, you'd tell me the truth."

Imagine how different this exchange might be if the listener had responded this way:

"I had expected you to call me the night before, so when you didn't I was worried that you were angry at me. When we met the next day, I was really nervous, and when you looked away from me, I was sure you *were* angry."

It is not uncommon for the validation for a *paranoia* to be another *paranoia*—like those Russian dolls that nest one inside the other. In this case, the first speaker might validate that she was actually hurt he hadn't called her; they had gotten their signals crossed about who was to call whom.

We sometimes call these articulations of intuition "paranoid fantasies," encouraging people to "go for broke," to elaborate stories that even to them seem improbable. The more material the receiver of a *paranoia* hears, the more clues she has to where the kernel of truth lies. Validating a *paranoia*—finding the link between two (or more) people's realities—is an extraordinarily powerful human interaction. Not knowing is among the most injurious states we must often endure. In a creative effort to make sense of what we perceive, *paranoia* as a common human response to assumptions can become clinical paranoia—a diagnosable instance of insanity. Many years ago, I worked in a state psychiatric institution, in the old days before anti-psychotic medication was available. Two thousand patients were warehoused for life in barrack-like wards. Sometimes, tracking down the genesis of a fixed *paranoia*, or even creating an alternative story speculatively, allowed people to let go of their troubled ideas. I remember one woman who was sure her neighbors had been poisoning her orange juice. She was diagnosed and committed and had sat on a ward for many years. As I got to know her, she told me a story of conflict with these neighbors over a property line issue. Having no clear legal documentation, the neighbors had generated nasty rumors about her in the community. When I suggested the kernel of truth in her *paranoia* may have been that they had poisoned her reputation, not her orange juice, she was very ready to accept that explanation. She became open to therapy, her "psychosis" steadily improved, and she was able to be discharged a few months later.

There is a gender aspect to the phenomenon of *paranoia*. Intuition serves a social function. Modern industrial society structures a distinct separation between domestic and occupational life. We go to work in places that are worlds with little or no relationship to home. (Of course, the internet age has enabled more and more people to work from home, raising another whole set of issues.) The things we do at work may have little or no relationship to who we are as individuals. We create objects we do not ourselves use or provide services for people we do not know. We work long hours. When we return home, we may be tuned out to our loved ones, out of sorts with our own inner emotional lives, restless and exhausted. We drink or smoke or veg in front of a screen. Relationships at home suffer. Very commonly, one person—more often than not a woman, although increasingly as our cultures of gender transform, perhaps a man—tries to reconnect by exercising skillful intuition. "What's the matter? Are you angry at me?" "Are you tired? Would you like a foot rub?" "How was your day? Will you tell me what's troubling you?" Having been assigned the role of intuitive nurturer, emotionally-expressive individuals, still most often women, then may be told they are crazy for imagining the things they pick up. And indeed, the assignment of such emotional work, an uphill slog, may well make women cranky. Rolling the boulder uphill evening after evening is a recipe for burnout, and burnout often takes an irritable form. Being judged harshly, and in psychiatric terms, for doing what women are carefully socialized to do, itself becomes a source of oppression.

This analysis may be broadly drawn, but it suggests a dynamic that commonly occurs in mediation: paranoid fantasy grown beyond the bounds of comprehension is very familiar. When a mediatee articulates a *paranoia*, the mediator works intently to help the listener locate and speak a kernel of truth, before identifying inaccuracies. Sometimes it takes some detective work to figure out what the truth is. The questions the mediator asks, the reflection stimulated for the one trying to give validation, the process of unpacking an important piece of the conflict, are invaluable.

All that, of course, requires an expansive amount of time. "I-statements" are brief and fast; *paranoias* can be time consuming. Time is a central facet of effective mediation. To rush the process is to invite exacerbating discord. Not only do people need the experience of full expression, but the content of what they express—the events that have caused them distress—are the raw material from which to form an understanding of the truest and deepest reasons for conflict.

When the radical therapy collective began mediation as a self-help tool, learning was a primary goal. After some time, as clients began to ask for mediation to be available as a service, the educational aspect of it continued to be important. So, while people are expressing themselves for the dual purposes of discharging emotional energy and revealing fully their experience of the issues, the mediator is also teaching skills. The idea is for mediators to work toward our own obsolescence. If the tools we use are useful, then they can be learned and used at will without need for professional intervention.

More than once, Bernal mediation folks called me before a meeting to get help formulating something they needed to work through with another member of the group. Before long, people voluntarily spoke up before trying to conduct business to give held feelings and check out *paranoias*. Getting a bit ahead of the story, a subset of those involved in the Bernal mediation went on to form a task force to implement the consensus reached by the whole group. In an impressive demonstration of using learned skills, people time and time again worked through potentially divisive moments, speaking what they felt and going on to work through different opinions respectfully and effectively. When the first designs were presented by the artists chosen to implement the consensus agreement, Giulio was worried that references to the old mural were inadequately represented. Brandon disagreed, believing the presence of a few images on the west wall were sufficient. As Giulio reflected on his childhood associations with the mural, the group moved to a reconsideration, in the end revising the offered design to include two meaningful elements of the Cortland portion of the mural. The creativity of that process strengthened the artwork, and served once again to draw the task force members closer together. When later they suffered a setback in the work, they dealt with it with both kindness and unanimity.

## Analysis: Writing a New Story

Conflict intervention modalities use a variety of approaches by which the mediator intervenes to shift the dynamics of conflict. Volunteer community mediators, for example, may engage in "active listening," saying back to participants what they hear them say as a way to acknowledge and ascertain the clarity of statements. What mediators make of those statements is left strictly unsaid. Other mediators may reframe statements, echoing what participants have said without the emotionality or judgment in the original articulation. In most modalities, mediators ask questions, which may range from informational to leading. "How much did you pay for it?" is very different from "What led you to decide to pay that amount for it?" In either case, the question more or less seriously influences the course of dialogue.

My approach is a good deal more direct and intentional. I believe that people in conflict are generally open to—indeed, hoping for—new, more constructive ways to think about what they are going through. They welcome analytic tools that aid in creating constructive change. After the subjective exchange of feelings, I offer a new story that brings into a unitary framework the disparate stories told so far. Mediators debate the perils of unduly influencing their clients; the idea is to mediate process, not content. I think the two are inseparable, and I have found over the years that people are very able to participate fully in the process of analyzing their conflicts. If some idea I suggest doesn't ring true, they offer correction—especially since I encourage them to do just that. I don't tell people I know better than they what's going on for them. I offer one possible account and invite them to discuss it with me until, together, we've created an understanding that rings true to everyone.

One way I think about this process is in terms of epistemology, the nature of knowledge. Postmodern theorists believe that there is no hard and fast reality, that all things are relative and we can only see things from the perspective of our own standpoint. Positivists, on the other hand, insist that the real world is concrete and describable—there is a reality that stays fixed, whether we can in a given moment perceive it or not. This debate is another I believe to be flawed. It needlessly divides up the world into oppositions. One of the joys of mediating is the opportunity to both honor important differences in the ways people experience a single, shared moment, and then to bring those disparate experiences into dynamic relationship with each other by accounting for them and molding them into a coherent third narrative. Think, for instance, of the moment Dan and Darcy saw the car depicted in the mural so differently. Dan opened a whole new level of communication when he said, "I'm a stereotype. No matter what I do, I'll always be a stereotype." Darcy's open response ("I don't understand. Please, please explain it.") joined in the process of expanding consciousness instrumentally. By plumbing those differences in viewing the image of the car, I was able to offer a story of cultural domination, unintentional racism, the pain of stereotyping, and, most importantly, of change and the nurturing of new affections. I brought to the process my own very political understanding of what had just happened, teaching a way of seeing race relations in a systemic context.

Often, as in this example, the analysis I offer is about power. I've laid out a way in which I think about power, as a dynamic occurring simultaneously in many different realms, from the internal to the social structural. That comprehensive model is useful in thinking about what's going on to generate the conflict at hand, and to sort crucial elements from secondary ones.

Always, a mediator working from this approach starts by naming the material reality that is the context for each person's reality. Three theoretical premises lie behind that choice: First, it is consistent with the wider assumption that subjective and objective realities are dynamically interconnected. Second, it suggests once again that what individuals think and feel makes sense in the context of objective circumstances. Third, in an individualist culture there is a strong tendency to overlook the environment in favor of psychological or moral concepts (which is a good example, by the way, of Gramscian theory, the idea that culture shapes consciousness in ways that induce individuals to consent to their own oppression (Gramsci 1997)). To first identify the material context in which subjective experience takes place is to base everything that follows in the project of connecting all the pieces of the conflict. It says there is something real and dignified about which to fight, that people are neither bad nor misguided in struggling for their interests.

In the Bernal mediation, progress was made when we looked beyond the obvious statements to deeper meanings. "Don't take away my mural!" raised the question of what the individual had experienced that so animated the passion with which he made that statement. What meaning did the mural hold and *for what material reason*? When Giulio introduced the word *entitlement* in the Bernal mediation, and Brandon the word *standing*, each was evoking a relationship to community, home, family, upward or downward economic mobility, and more. Giulio might have been seen to be claiming a sense of ownership of the neighborhood, based on his family's longevity living there, but in fact he was instead speaking about a way people behaved toward him. Brandon may have been claiming a right, but instead he was suggesting his need to create a warm community within which to raise his children and wondering whether he had the power to do that. Not surprisingly, unpacking the meanings and the lived realities behind those two words—entitlement and standing—led to a recognition that, on some level, both were asking for respectful and engaged community relations, and at the same time that each came to that request from a very different lived experience and material reality, expressing what they sought in very different cultural vocabularies.

What follows understanding closely, however, is critique of the ways in which people have been expressing their experience. As mediators, we need to be forthright in pointing out how interpersonal behaviors have inflamed and often obscured the heart of what needs to be solved. The task is to widen the lens of analysis to encompass the larger material context, and at the same time to narrow the lens to understand in detail the immediate interpersonal behaviors of the individuals involved.

After the Bernal mediatees had cleared the air, articulating vividly the emotionally-laden events that had hardened positions, it was possible for Cynthia and me to diagram the contexts and relationships within which the immediate dispute nested. We spoke to the history of earlier disputes, never deeply resolved but leaving a segment of the community, represented by Mauricio, hurt and disgruntled. We spoke about city politics that had contributed to that outcome, and we "nested" that history in the larger history of neighborhood economic changes that threatened earlier cultural modes of conducting community.

Economic changes in the city and therefore the neighborhood were bringing into association people with little knowledge of each other's lives. Their cultural dissimilarities included assumptions about the uses of public space. For some, playing in the street was a very normal source of enjoyment. For others, however, a proper home environment was quiet and private. Moreover, different segments of the community held different interests. Some "old-timers" mourned a way of life as well as the loss of friends whose families had been forced to move away as the cost of living in the neighborhood outstripped their means. Change was a bad thing, infringing on their contentment. Newer settlers in the neighborhood, though, had often invested their entire financial reserves in buying their homes. They hoped and prayed the value of their property would increase over time; their personal economic well-being depended on gentrification, exactly those changes that harmed others' quality of life. So both culture and socioeconomic structure promoted the clash.

Into this charged atmosphere was dropped the library renovation. Libraries tend to be shared public spaces, valued and utilized across economic and ethnic lines. Both old-timers and newcomers felt a sense of attachment to the library. What to some in the mediation was an essential aspect to that institution—a mural arising from their own youths—to others was defacement. Without daily interaction and an understanding of the material and cultural factors shaping their reactions, people spoke out in unguarded ways. Darcy heard expressions of hurt and anger because she had publicly referred to the mural as "ugly." Mauricio listened to the consequences of his calling people "racist" as fellow Bernal-ites spoke of their surprise, hurt, and outrage.

To describe the history of the conflict in terms of nesting dynamics, also noting escalatory behaviors and understanding them in terms of experiences neither person could otherwise know about the other, all in the context of changes taking place beyond either's power to intervene, helps enormously to de-personalize the dispute and open territory for change. If the ways people behave in a conflict are seen as something that can be intentionally altered, then direct criticism delivered in a respectfully nurturing way widens the chances of enduring change.

One of the most common dynamics that arises in interpersonal and organizational conflicts is, paradoxically, grounded in generosity and a desire to help. It is described by a concept called the "rescue triangle." A tool for understanding the phenomenon of resentment that follows self-sacrifice, it describes three roles that people familiarly play: Rescuer, Victim, Persecutor. To Rescue is to do more than your fair share of the work in a given context, or to do things you really don't want to do. We Rescue because we view someone as being a Victim, an assessment with which the person in that role may agree. A Victim is someone who believes his or her power to be less than it truly is. She feels helpless in the face of particular tasks or needs, or is not aware of the need itself. To be less than powerful to take care of oneself is a thankless experience. In discomfort, we rebel, Persecuting those particularly who remind us we are not capable by overreaching to help.

Meanwhile, the Rescuer burns out from trying to do the impossible, which is to help in a way that communicates an absence of belief in the Victim's potential to partner in the activity. Think about a parent who cooks perfectly healthful meals on the theory that she knows her child's nutritional needs better than the child. The child, who has perhaps learned to override his body's signals about what is healthy to consume, under the dual assaults of "mother-knows-best" and TV commercials, resents having something as fundamental as appetite controlled by the parent. And so he rebels, refusing to eat the prepared meal, perhaps refusing to sit at the family table at all. Parent moves rapidly around the Triangle, becoming increasingly worried, angry, exhausted, and, in the end all the more authoritarian and punitive. In the process, she reinscribes the lesson that the child is wrong (and perhaps bad), inviting more feelings of powerlessness for all concerned.

This model is helpful because it is one of the very few psychological constructs that analyzes emotional and interpersonal experiences in terms of power. Leadership in public contexts can easily fall into a Rescue pattern. Both Mauricio and Darcy became increasingly hostile as they took on more and more responsibility for mobilizing and speaking for "their people." Dedication to a good cause can lead to burnout and behaviors that inflame rather than constructively address problems. Similar dynamics happen in all sorts of settings, from the family dinner table to the boardroom. It happens in a particular structural setting: scarcity of resources. Imagine, for instance, how different the dinner table example might be if there were lots of other adults around to cook lots of different foods, to observe what kids liked to eat, to invite them to have a role in choosing and preparing menus. There would be time to let kids play out a very common juvenile pattern of desiring different food groups on different days in an environment of leisure and relaxation.

### Negotiation: Swings and Crunches

Emotional expression and analytic understanding are preludes to finding solutions. All conflict intervention needs is to be based on a conviction that there is something worth fighting for at the heart of the matter. Having cleared the air and identified what essential contradictions are dividing the combatants, the next step is to negotiate change.

As I wrote in an earlier chapter, our approach to conflict intervention declines to be positioned on either side of the relationship-versus-settlement controversy within the field. The two are inextricably interwoven. On a theoretical level, a social constructivist orientation suggests that material reality frames human consciousness. Modern industrial cultures, however, create dualistic oppositions between the two realms, and these divisions show up in mediation. Legal specialists may seek to manage emotion in order to keep it from interfering with a process of negotiated settlement. Therapeutically oriented mediators may rest content with a frank expression of feelings, believing that the unusual experience of getting a full hearing is sufficiently "empowering" to constitute success.

But if the starting assumption is that there is no separation between subjectivity and objectivity, then it becomes possible, and necessary, to ask several key questions. Two or more people may be reporting experiences that seem totally opposed: "It happened!" "No, it didn't!" If no one is lying and no one is crazy, then there's a mystery to be solved. Inquiry into the details of each person's experience may realign their realities. Exploring their interpretations, the meanings they made of what they each perceived happening, creates a common framework within which to reconcile differing standpoints. Often, these explorations help to articulate differing worldviews, cultural acknowledgment that may prompt a re-examination of interests in light of deeper awareness of underlying needs and wants.

This process of discovery says to people that their world adds up. Their reality makes sense. How they see things is neither right nor wrong, but it is important. This validation, both from opponents and from a person with authority, the mediator, allows for a relaxation of tensions—a little bit.

Beyond that point, however, what relaxes tension is resolution. By this point, there has probably been a shift in power relations. People are not simply negotiating changes "out there," but are experiencing changes in relationship "in the room." In a very useful volume edited by Deborah Kolb, *When Talk Works* (1997), mediators engaging in a wide variety of types of work are interviewed and their work described by a writer. One mediator makes the clear statement that power imbalances must be "left at the door"—that is, resolved before people begin the process of mediation. Another talks about how imbalances are evened out "at the table." I see both as containing some truth and much error. Imbalances need to be specified. Are they about organizational roles, or based in social identities, or seated in serious economic discrepancies? How willing are people to commit to equality of rights, and therefore to foregoing possible deployments of power? If a supervisor involved in an employment dispute holds the power to summarily fire a supervisee, then mediation can only proceed if there is some reasonable assurance that the conversation is privileged. On the other hand, I've done these mediations when the employee is so near quitting if things don't get better that she's willing to take the risk of termination. But a worker who cannot afford to risk his job might be foolish to "sit at a balanced table," for the table is inevitably tilted at what for him is a dangerous angle.

At the same time, power is, as I've said elsewhere, dynamic. The experience of equal expression, of dignifying responses by a mediator and validation by an opponent, of negotiation protected by a mediator's advocacy for a just solution, brings about a shift. Harm can be done if people enter into a negotiation of change while any significant imbalance in power still exists. My objective is never simply to settle the issue at hand; it is to help people build a sufficiently cooperative relationship that they can construct an *enduring* solution. They must have reached an emotional and attitudinal place from which they can negotiate with a will to share the gains. That is, each must truly believe that his or her own well-being depends on the other's well-being, and vice versa.

Let me draw out implications of the contrast between adversarial and cooperative negotiation. So much has been written about "win-win" negotiation that I need not belabor the distinction. But there are some important characteristics of cooperative negotiation that I think may not be widely understood:

First, intention to negotiate fairly is not the same as an ability to negotiate fairly. By "ability," I mean power. If Mauricio had begun to negotiate at the beginning of the library renovation process, he would almost certainly have lost his objective. Those whose cultural aesthetic was dominant enjoyed commensurate political access. Moreover, they had confidence to speak out in public forums and a will to advocate for what they wanted. Darcy owned a store in a very central location—central from both a geographic and a cultural standpoint—and she could, with the best of intentions, use her shop as an organizing tool. She put notices in the window, sponsored a petition, talked with people, and mobilized public opinion that, in her world, already ran heavily against the murals. Darcy and her allies showed up at policy-making meetings, speaking the language in which official business was conducted.

Mauricio, on the other hand, had potential power to mobilize his own troops. But without his fanning the flames, his followers were unlikely to act. Many were Spanish speakers, uncomfortable in all-English settings. They tended to assume their community would not "win" in a public fight—witness the previous lost battle to keep the pre-school in the library building. They had seen their numbers in the community wane, while those of the people they assumed were lobbying against the murals were growing.

To sit at a table prematurely, therefore, was for Mauricio to negotiate at a disadvantage. What he did, instead, was to stir passions by broadcasting his own feelings on the issue. He organized groups of young men to show up at commission meetings. He raised money and bought billboards and got the attention of the media. Aggregating the power to negotiate meant for him making trouble. He needed to make it more problematic for city authorities to erase the murals than to keep them.

Once that had happened, however, there was so much bad blood produced that negotiating had become impossible. It was only after three months of mediation had taken place that people could recognize each other's humanity and meet with sufficient respect for each other's rights and sufficient recognition of each other's power that a solution could be created.

The first principle of cooperative negotiation is that it depends on equal rights and equal power.

Second, a cooperatively achieved settlement is never finished. It is always a work in progress. After the consensus statement had been written, agreed to, and celebrated, Amy and others had second thoughts. We could have said, "Too bad, you should have thought of that sooner." But had we done so, the agreement would not have held. Again, the objective is not temporary peace but rather enduring change. When we wearily returned to the table, we had deeper insight into some aspects of the matter and we could write a better consensus.

Successful mediation has a momentum and a joy to it. By the time negotiation takes place, hearts are open and imaginations engaged. People may well, in the rush of good feeling, agree to something that seems good and right. But by next morning's light, it is clearly inadequate. The agreement, then, needs to be renegotiated. Often, second thoughts are thought to be betrayals. I urge people to see them as moments of constructive improvement. The only agreement that needs never to change is the agreement to make change collaboratively. In other words, call your fellow negotiator back to the table, but never simply renege or unilaterally change the agreement.

### Consensus

With these conditions, cooperative negotiation follows a few rules. These are rules of cooperative behavior generally as they were articulated by the early founders of radical therapy:

1) Honesty: no secrets or lies. Any information withheld is, in this context, a secret or, more provocatively, a lie of omission. Information is power; the one who knows holds power the other lacks. In that imbalance, a lasting negotiated outcome is imperiled.

2) Clarity about one's interests: in other words, no "Rescue." If you generously allow the other's needs to take precedence over your own, eventually you will feel victimized and become unwilling to uphold the agreement.

3) Persuasion rather than coercion: no "power plays," which means abjuring any action intended to make another person do something he or she would not otherwise willingly do.

These three rules are deceptively simple, but in practice they are operational steps toward constructing truly collaborative relationships. I've outlined them in a very specific context: a context in which there exists a clear recognition of mutual rights and powers, and clear enough relationships that people can truly actualize these attitudes and behaviors. In other circumstances, where power is contested and rights are denied, to tell the truth or privilege another's interests as well as one's own, can be a recipe for disadvantage. You may not, for instance, want to tell the absolute truth to someone who can fire you from your job, or to someone holding a gun to your head—or even a parent with a will to withhold your allowance if she disapproves of the truth you tell. But in mediation, these cooperative behaviors are in the interest of all parties who have made their way to negotiation—or else the mediation has failed to make possible a truly collaborative outcome. The record of divorce mediation, for example, is speckled with examples: couples pressured by courts to "mediate" settlements under conditions of inequality and scarcity that result in unjust outcomes to one or both parties.

## Restoring Human Connection in the End

By the time agreement has been reached, everyone is generally ready to go home, the mediator included. But we're not done yet. There are two final steps: making a plan for implementation and sharing recognition.

The only good advice about making a plan is to make it detailed. What needs to be done? Who exactly will do what part of it? What does each person need in order to do what she or he is committing to do? How will each person actually materialize the resources and support they need? Leave as little as possible to the imagination. Translate good intentions into reality and use those last ounces of creative juice to figure out how to manifest whatever is needed.

At this point, if not earlier, apologies are sometimes in order. I don't count apologizing as a necessary part of conflict intervention. Sometimes, it is clearly required if relationships are to be restored. Has one individual done something that caused harm to another? If so, then a good apology consists of three parts: a recognition of the harm done, a convincing statement of intent never to do such harm again, and a description of what has changed that makes it likely that the person harmed can trust it will not happen again. Too often, apologies lack that last part. It's easy to say, "I'm sorry I harmed you and I don't intend to do it again." But if most harm is done not with intention but instead as a result of particular circumstances and dynamics, then some new learning or resources or conditions are needed for apology to be believable. Apologies not grounded in change become moral statements defining someone as perpetrator and someone else as victim. Neither definition is useful, in the sense that punishment does not predict safety. Indeed, too often punishment stimulates renewed resentment, resistance, and misdeed. I'm not talking here of severe crimes, of rape or murder or assault. In those cases, mediation would not be a possibility. But in situations amenable to mediation, change is far more valuable than moral accountability.

Finally, we generally end mediation with "strokes"—more jargon indicating a positive statement of recognition. To "speak the love" is equally important in organizational or civic mediations as it is in intimate ones. Claude Steiner (2009, 43–49) coined the notion of a "stroke economy." By that he meant that there is a false scarcity of strokes. In most cultures, we learn a set of rules that limit expressions of appreciation, affection, acknowledgment. We are told not to say them lest people think we are maneuvering for some gain; not to accept them lest people think we are vain; not to ask for them lest people think we are needy; not to reject them (when they are actually disguised injunctions, such as "You are so sweet" when a woman wants acknowledgment for being strong, or "You are so strong" when a man wants to be appreciated for his sweet insightfulness); and finally don't stroke yourself, a pervasive, trans-cultural injunction against boasting.

As a result, we lack reflections of our most positive selves, and so we keep trying harder to "win" recognition at the same time that we hide behind walls called "privacy" in fear of others' judgments. The stroke economy begets alienation and competition; it constructs a world of depressed and anxious individuals. No wonder psychoactive pharmaceuticals attract such profits!

To end the hard work of conflict resolution with an exchange of strokes is therefore to reap rewards and to rebuild connections. It is easy to skip this step out of fatigue or shyness or embarrassment, but it is as important as anything else that has happened.

# 13

# Conclusions and Recommendations

CONFLICT INTERVENTION as a profession has a very short history. Conflict itself, of course, is as old as human memory stretches. Traditions of intervention existed long before the days when money changed hands for the service. Grandmothers, clergy, wise and friendly neighbors were regularly called upon to help people come to terms in the midst of disputes.

All these interveners lived in some sort of relationship to those they assisted. As our community links have weakened, professional services have increasingly taken the place of turning to known folks in times of trouble. We go to therapists for solace rather than loving aunts, physicians for childbirth rather than nearby midwives, lawyers for advocacy when marriages break apart rather than rabbis or priests.

Professions require boundaries; if the labor of the practitioner commands money, then something must distinguish that individual from the common run of humanity. And so we get degrees and licenses, credentials and ethical rules. In turn, each of these demarcations rests on proven expertise in a body of knowledge. In order to hold many people to one common standard, a canon is necessary: one set of ideas and practices on which applicants to the profession can be tested. The diversity of approaches that span the inclinations of grandmothers and rabbis is gradually squeezed out of acceptability. The law, for instance, is the law is the law. There is one law for everyone. But if you attend any appellate court process, you will hear debated different interpretations of law, and underlying those differences may lie profound differences of legal philosophy. Even more so in medicine; while every practicing MD in a state has passed the same licensing examination, doctors may apply a variety of approaches: homeopathy, acupuncture, ayurveda, or many other systems of understanding the human body and its healing, none of them tested for medical licensure.

The canon therefore privileges particular bodies of knowledge while promoting the belief that there is in fact only one right way to understand the subject. Conflict resolution is not as far along as law and medicine in professionalizing, but many practitioners seek to be on that path—with some good reason. Professionalization creates means to enforce standards of quality. It both demands that practitioners have undergone training that is accepted as valid, and it also allows for intervention should a particular practitioner do harm to clients. The downside, however, is that it also creates a dominant methodology, legitimizing one set of understandings over others.

There is thus an underlying conflict in the world of conflict resolvers: is it a good thing or a bad thing to promote professionalization? Is the loss of diversity compensated by gains in quality? Which, of course, raises another question: who is to decide what quality is? Which set of standards becomes official is not accidental. In general, the people who create legitimate knowledge in a field are those whose ideas most conform to beliefs in the dominant culture. Roberto Chené, an unconventional and highly respected Chicano practitioner, often says the problem of multiculturalism is not difference but domination (Chené 2008). A politic of knowledge is created, and it replicates the politic of identity in society at large. The more the legitimized modes of understanding and working narrow to a mainstream few, the more people from nondominant cultures become delegitimized as professionals. With their work either missing or, more commonly, happening without acknowledgment, under-researched and unknown, new entrants to the field are required to study and learn ways of thinking and acting that are more and more foreign to them. They therefore too often drop out, partly because the worth of their culturally-informed inclinations are demeaned, and partly because entry into paid work looms dauntingly difficult.

I believe those of us who do the work of conflict intervention, and those who wish to do it as well, need to cast a critical eye on what we have wrought. We need to regard with distrust anything that encourages us to accept as axiomatic particular manifestations of the work, as if there is one right way or one size that fits all. As I near the end of this story of the Bernal mediation, I worry that I may promote exactly that fallacy. The Bernal mediation succeeded for a set of clear reasons. If one of them was my skill, I say, with no undue humility, my contribution was only one thread in a particularly colorful weave.

I end, therefore, with an attempt to build a more nuanced frame on which to craft the tapestry of mediation.

## Is Conflict Resolution a Movement or a Methodology?

I often hear people speak of conflict resolution as intrinsically a superior way to handle conflict. Referencing the moral and practical benefits of nonviolent collaboration, these advocates of mediated processes plead passionately that disputants use them in any and all conflict situations. I appreciate the vigor and idealism of this position, even as I fear some of its consequences.

We in western societies live in cultures deeply rooted in competitive individualism. Fighting to win is a value reflected in team sports, academic rankings, career advancement, consumer marketing, and popular TV shows that promise fame and fortune to successful contestants. To challenge that pervasive worldview by promoting alternatives to conducting conflict in adversarial ways is wholly commendable. Many mediators and other conflict interveners might, in another time, have been leading social uprisings like those of the 1960s, or the more recent Arab Spring. But in the West today, such movements are lacking. After the civil rights, feminist, free speech, and other challenges abated in the 1980s, some participants, disappointed in the results of their ardent actions, turned to conflict resolution as a value-based way to make a difference. If they had been unable to change things on the big platform of social progress, they could make an impact at the small table mediating face-to-face conflicts. Many of the early theorists—people like Lou Kriesberg, Margaret Herrman, and Paul Wahrhaftig—had roots as activists. The work they contributed was principled and optimistic.

Precisely because it was often enough also effective, it became more and more institutionalized. Consider divorce mediation, for instance. In the early 1970s, we who were evolving radical therapy mediated divorcing couples fairly often, and we trained others in doing the work. Increasingly—and I admit, much to my relief!—lawyers took over the work. I still mediate relational issues in the process of divorce, especially co-parenting tensions. But the settlement-oriented work has moved on primarily to attorneys, many of whom call themselves "lapsed lawyers" because they so prefer the heart-healing collaborative work to hostile litigation.

In the beginning, people who sought out mediation were aware of its meaning and ready to work cooperatively. The process was, by definition, voluntary. Nowadays, most court systems require divorcing couples to try to reach settlement through mediation before appealing to the judge. Whatever the emotional state of disrepair in their relationship, people are pressured, more or less subtly, to come to agreement. The work takes place in a time of high duress, filled with pain and uncertainty. When stressed, most of us rely on familiar ways to behave. Cultural dynamics are therefore prevalent in these situations. Long ago, when divorce mediation was first becoming a frequent modality, Laura Nader wrote a searing critique of the ways it disadvantaged women (Nader 1988). In today's compulsory circumstances, I find on anecdotal levels her concerns are borne out. Women more often negotiate with a conciliatory eye to future relationships, while men, especially those used to controlling financial resources, play to protect what they believe they've earned and therefore deserve to control. The value of women's contribution to the amassing of assets—the unpaid labor of housework and childcare, the work at jobs in traditionally women's occupations that reap lower wages than men's for comparable work—still tends to disappear from the reckoning in many settlement negotiations. So even when women argue for their economic rights, the structure of the conversation is all too often men-in-possession versus women-making-claims.

Similarly, dynamics of race enter into mediation outcomes. There is some—but not sufficient—research showing that people reared in more collectivist cultures appreciate collaborative processes more than judicial ones, but fare less well in their outcomes. More subtle issues of race may also intrude. For example, in one business partnership dissolution (not one I mediated; I advised one of the participants, instead) my client, a black, immigrant woman, spoke again and again of the reasons why she brought in fewer new customers than her white male partner. They worked in a traditionally male and very white technical field. Her credibility as an expert was routinely questioned, even though she was a star among her colleagues. She provided a greater-than-even share of the services their small company rendered, but in the end the dissolution agreement, negotiated with a white male mediator, rested on the number of contracts written, disadvantaging her bottom line. For her, the principles involved were contextual, social, qualitative, and complex. For the two men, they were quantitative and unarguable.

Mediation is therefore not a panacea. Under circumstances of relative disadvantage and privilege, neutral intervention by a professionally-trained practitioner may be harmful. The unintended consequences may exactly oppose the value-based motivations of the provider. The context for collaborative decision-making is always equality of power. Power, as I've written, is exceedingly complex and dynamic. To enter into a process without sufficiently understanding the social structural context, the cultures involved, and the extenuating circumstances of the individuals, is hazardous.

### What's So Special about Bernal?

Why, then, did the Bernal mediation work so well? Lots of the dynamics I've just listed were evident. There was reason to suspect the existence of power imbalances with significant consequence. Multicultural dynamics of strife were rampant and complex with people representing a wide variety of heritages and identities: Latino, African-American, bi-racial Filipino-Italian, white Protestant, Jewish; gay and straight; parenting and not; young and old; male and female. The fault lines of possible cultural domination were many. The issue itself was classically zero-sum: one wall, two very different well-argued wishes for what went on it.

I believe there were several prominent features that nonetheless made success possible:

First, the fight had gone on long enough to accomplish two ends: the segment of the community that believed itself to be most disadvantaged had gained power by organizing, and everyone was so battle weary that the desire for resolution ran strong in the land.

People of color, primarily people of color with Latino heritage, might otherwise have been disadvantaged on several levels. They were losing presence in the neighborhood as the price of housing forced them out. This factor melded issues of culture and race with dynamics of class. Interestingly, on the basis of identity they were well represented in the institutional seats of power. The supervisor, the city librarian, and the director of the San Francisco Arts Commission all shared identity with those campaigning to save the mural. But those alliances did not necessary read as reliable in the context of class. Given historic experiences of colonization echoed in a modern key by repeated incidents of exclusion from seats of political power, many Latino residents doubted the reliability of support from officials even when they shared identity.

What the Latino community did have was determined leadership in the person of Mauricio Vela. Mauricio deployed the one tactic most calculated to give his side voice: he refused to go away. Also, as the fight went on, he became more and more personally passionate about it, and his constituency became committed to the fight to a commensurate degree. So Mauricio and those for whom he spoke entered the picture of the mediation with a great deal of power, evidenced among other ways by the tentativeness with which the group of people who first briefed me introduced his name.

On the other side, the New Deal for Bernal people moved comfortably in the realm of policymaking. They included politically engaged leaders like Darcy Lee, who had extensive experience transacting successfully in official worlds as a business owner and leader of the Cortland merchants. Others held similarly respected positions; they directed public institutions, sat on boards of community organizations, had long histories of participating in public discourse. What undercut their power was the fact that the decision-making process was so unclear at first. They had presented a powerful case to the library commission, only to have the city attorney rule that the commission had no jurisdiction. Fogginess at the level of government shook the familiar ground under those whose comfort speaking in the language of official discourse was greater.

By the time Supervisor Campos initiated the mediation, the two vocal sides were well matched. While everyone experienced themselves as less powerful at certain moments in the process, over time they discovered the equality of their voices and were able to speak for their needs, rights, and interests in potent ways. As their relationships thus deepened—nothing so powerfully opens the heart as the experience of speaking truth and being heard—each individual came genuinely to feel committed to protecting the interests of every other individual. Sometimes that dedication slipped in the heat of controversy over a particular detail, but each time, through the same processes of honest dialogue, the group worked through the difficulty and re-accessed that sense of unified purpose.

The second factor that aided success was the unequivocal belief by official city leaders that the dispute needed to be resolved within the community. Whatever partisan political agendas might have been in play years earlier had fallen away, partly I suspect through attrition, but also because the current leadership was progressive. Both David Campos, the supervisor, and Luis Herrera, the city librarian, were clearly committed to the notion that the highest value was community reconciliation and autonomy, whatever outcome they might otherwise have desired. If they had competing interests, they kept them thoroughly out of the process. The interests negotiated in the mediation were, therefore, present in the room. In many cases, participants at the table bring with them influences from and obligations to people not in the room. That condition is natural; we all have multiple social and political linkages, and we cannot easily divorce ourselves from such collective commitments. But in the Bernal mediation, we had the very good fortune of not having to deal with outside forces distorting the process at key and unfortunate moments. The only slight experience in this domain came not from an official and therefore powerful source, but from the artist who painted out his own mural, an individual act that could be reasonably neutralized as the momentum of the mediation for consensus swelled.

The third reason the Bernal mediation was so effective had to do with my willingness to play multiple roles, and with the resulting absence of professional distance between mediator and mediatees. It was only through the network of my relationships with people in the community that I was able to access the broad range of people I interviewed and to choose those who eventually took part so wisely. Wisdom sprang not from my intellect, or even my intuition, although both may have played some role. Instead, I was informed by years of relationship in the community. Those years also legitimized me both to the people at the table and, afterward, to those who were not.

At many points the process might have stalemated had I not seen my job in terms of multiple roles. I counseled Mauricio, talking through his dilemma about whether the time was right to mediate. I organized by meeting with impatient and doubtful groups of community members. I educated by teaching tools and concepts, such as Rescue and Nested Theory. I engaged in conscious anti-racism work, offering new ways to understand dynamics at moments like Dan and Darcy's hard moment over the vintage car. I gave personal criticism, in a respectful and loving way, when people acted in ways that escalated conflict. I facilitated community meetings in the aftermath of the mediation. And throughout, I encouraged, reminded, nagged, nurtured, reframed—in short, performed whatever acts of leadership seemed necessary.

When conflict interveners define their role as neutral, they eliminate the flexibility demanded by work as complex as the Bernal mediation. I believe the formulation of neutrality to be unnecessarily one-dimensional. If I truly believe that each person's interest lies in the satisfaction of all people's interests, then I can speak powerfully for any element in the dispute in the confidence that I am helping all. One day, while trying to teach this concept to students, I coined a new word: I claimed I was not impartial but "polypartial." I'd like to see polypartiality adopted as the standard of the field, because it necessitates a multidimensional understanding of both conflict and helpful intervention.

Last, but far from least, the Bernal mediation was made possible by my interactions with colleagues whose cultural backgrounds enriched my understanding of what was going on. Mediators these days commonly attend some form of cultural competency training. They might spend as much as forty hours at the task, although often it is far less. In that time, they get a smattering of instruction about how to interact with different cultural groups. Of necessity, the learning is thin. The great privilege I've had to live in a culture so very dissimilar to my own (India, rather than the United States for many years; San Francisco, rather than Texas for many more) and to be tutored by my colleagues of color (especially those working with me at the Practitioners Research and Scholarship Institute) has, over many years, challenged the worldview with which I was endowed. There's a bumper sticker that says, "Don't believe everything you think." I had the very good fortune to learn that lesson at a young age. It takes support, openness, and, most importantly, opportunity to cross cultural boundaries in ways that reach the fundamentals. One such opportunity is co-mediating with colleagues in a way that truly co-creates the work from start to finish.

Understanding culture is a matter not of rituals and customs but of worldviews. Rather than cultural competency trainings, I believe we need cultural travelers to do the work of multicultural conflict intervention. (I also believe all conflict is multicultural, involving ways of making meaning and negotiating power.) Cultural travelers may never leave home, but they are on an endless journey of discovery, attentive to every new experience of unfamiliar ways of thinking. They inquire rather than assume. They stretch to put themselves inside the mindset of people different from themselves. They welcome learning from their clients. They withstand the discomfort of not understanding, knowing also the joy of cultural enlightenment.

## Recommendations for Conflict Interveners

I end with a few recommendations for the field. Insofar as we are becoming a profession, we do not need to do things the way other modern professions have done them. We can ensure quality without adopting judicial forms of overview and while preserving diversity of approaches appropriate to the particular people with whom we work. Some ideas, intended to stimulate discussion and invention:

  • *Train in apprenticeship.* The tools of mediating can be taught in reasonably brief workshops, but to become skillful takes experience. I frequently hear would-be mediators complain that after having gone through the requisite number of hours of training, they still can't find opportunities to actually practice the work. Community mediation centers do offer some possibilities to volunteers, but seemingly there is more desire for training than there is demand for mediations. Panels of mediators, the model used by community boards in San Francisco, are helpful, partnering more experienced people with newcomers. Still, consistent mentoring is not necessarily available; again, the numbers don't match up and all too often, neither does the funding.

I teach mediation in two circumstances: at the University of California, Berkeley, and privately. The UC work is wonderful, and I get to do a two-week intensive every summer. A lot happens in those two weeks. Students come from all over the world, teaching me as much as I teach them. Occasionally, someone goes on to forge a career in conflict intervention. More often, students tell me the learning benefitted their own lives, but they don't become practitioners.

My private teaching is very different. With a colleague, I train apprentices. They sit in on the work we do, and also meet together as a group at regular intervals. Over time, they move from observing, to assisting, to leading the work. By the time—often three to five years later—that they launch on their own, they are skilled and capable.

  • *Make ongoing peer support and learning a requirement.* For many years, one criterion for being a radical therapist was meeting with peers in a weekly or bi-weekly peer supervision group. We talked in detail about the work we were doing, consulted about difficulties, strategized together how to handle hard problems, and learned from the collective experience in a way that was uniquely helpful. One year, at a conflict resolution conference, colleagues and I tried to bring mediators together in a similar way. Nobody came. The "foot language"—that is, the feet went elsewhere—testified, I thought, to fears about exposing ones inadequacies as a practitioner to one's peers. I was sympathetic: by definition, professions are competitive. Despite the use of the model by courts, and despite promotion of mediation by community and for-profit agencies as a better way to go about things, there still seem to be far more mediators than the market can support. At another conference of mediators where I recently did a keynote address, I asked the audience how many people were actually getting cases on a regular basis. Very few hands went up. I asked how many wanted to be earning their living substantially as mediators, and almost every hand went up. Conferences therefore become places to generate business. People come looking for referrals. Revealing that one doesn't know how to do something is not good marketing. Besides, we Americans are supposed to be expert in whatever endeavors we undertake. Not to know is to fail. Definitions of success breed secrecy. In the process, ongoing learning is short-circuited.

Imagine if every mediator could turn to a group of known peers for consultation and support. Imagine if that group used its own skills to work through competitiveness and build trust among themselves, so that asking for help could be seen as a mark of strength, not weakness. We would be practicing what we preach, that collaborative work works better.

▪ *Share knowledge across cultures with mutuality.* In our multicultural world, swimming easily in diverse cultural environments is essential. But the materials available for training mediators tend to privilege dominant culture, and the access of already-trained mediators to other worlds of meaning-making is disturbingly superficial.

Classically, those whose cultures are marginalized know more about those in the center than the other way around, an old story marginally improved by increased multicultural representations in today's media. We need to build literatures written by people of color and others whose knowledge is underrepresented. We need to seat research in places where the work is done in ways suited to the cultural idioms of the people served.

One excellent agency in southern California years ago tried to promote conflict resolution in a community of newly-arrived Asian immigrants, but the people they tried to serve wanted instead to be guided through the intricacies of conventional adjudication systems. As newcomers, they sensed they first needed to know the established systems before they were willing to trust alternatives. To understand those tensions would be invaluable learning for those of us who champion what we consider the more humane forms of intervention.

When the Practitioners Research and Scholarship Institute convened groups of practitioners of color to begin outlining an anthology, people gradually began to tell stories of how they *really* worked in the institutional settings where they were employed. "I don't tell anybody," they said, in a variety of ways, "because I'd be fired. But I don't do the stuff I was trained to do. Won't work with the people I work with. So when the door is closed, this is how I actually do things." Those stories are, in the words of political scientist James Scott, hidden transcripts (Scott 1992). We need to bring them into the light, publish them in the textbooks, use them in the trainings for court mediators and everyone else, for they contain knowledge just as useful to the mainstream as to particular groups. Every one of those stories was a tale of tailoring work to the people at the table, in the context of their particular ways of doing things, in their language. At the same time, they were inspiring accounts of guiding people to different kinds of conversations in which customs were challenged just enough to bring about collaborative results. All in all, they taught many crucial lessons about power, themes relevant to us all.

- *Create programs to train and support "barefoot mediators."*
I've emphasized several times the importance of my relationships in
the community. Had I been an outsider, a professional of standing
from somewhere else, something else positive might have resulted,
but I strongly believe that the depth and quality of the work was
facilitated by my lack of distance.

One outcome of the mediation was demonstrated at one of the
community meetings. A woman in the room was clearly disgruntled. Through body language and off-record sounds, she communicated very clearly that she was in disagreement. I thought I might be
needed to intervene, but before that moment came, Brandon quietly
approached her. He invited her to leave the room with him, heard
her out, engaged in dialogue with her, and promised to transmit her
grievances to the group as a whole. She was grateful, and she later
offered to work on the making of new art.

Brandon's good heart was something intrinsic to who he is, but
his skill in handling the conflict was something born of the conflict
transformation work he had experienced. I believe that transmitting
skills, including the confidence to intervene, is an important aspect
of all constructive conflict transformation. How much more powerful it might be if we actually trained natural leaders in the community before intervention were needed! I envision programs in which
people—youths, elders, shopkeepers, barbers—could volunteer to be
trained for readiness, and supported in ongoing ways when occasions
arose to use those skills.

In a sense, such training is already happening through community
mediation programs, but most of those programs (to my knowledge;
I'd be happy to learn of exceptions) construct their work in institutional ways, even though they intend to make neighbors available to
help neighbors. That is, clients come to them for help, there are formal
processes for intake, and mediators are trained in strict neutrality as
a way to ensure a certain quality to the work. Many of these agencies
provide great services, but I've heard trained volunteers bemoan the
scarcity of mediations to be done as they wait for word to get out.

What I'm imagining is more along the lines of a flying squad, a group of people who come to know about conflict because they are witnessing it, and who have a reputation for stepping forward and offering intervention. Their credibility would be based in their commonalities with the people they mediate. In Oakland, California, a man named Kevin Grant does an extreme version of this work. He intervenes when gangs are about to come to violent blows, and he is effective because he is himself an ex-con (Jones 2012).

# Afterword

HOW DO WE ASSESS the consequences of an intervention like the Bernal one? Formal means for evaluation are hard to come by. What constitutes success? Is it a continuing absence of conflict? Or is it more that future conflict is productive, creating change rather than harm? In a world as complex as ours, one person's progress may be another's injury, so even concepts of progress and injury are complicated. By the goals of the participants, the Bernal mediation was clearly a success. It moved the community beyond a seemingly intractable dispute. It restored friendly relations among many people who had been seriously at odds with each other. It even brought about a resolution to the immediate dispute, changing the physical face of the library itself.

As I write these concluding words, art is going up on the walls. The members of the task force formed out of the mediation group have continued to work together, losing one member to mortality, another to relocation, and gaining a couple of new participants. The group hired a splendid project manager, an accomplished woman named Gia Grant. Well experienced in the complexities of working with city agencies to produce new cultural forms, Gia guided the task force through mazes of tasks, raising sizeable amounts of money (with admirable support from Mayor Ed Lee), selecting and hiring artists, soliciting community input, and riding out the inevitable ups and downs of the process.

The ups have been many. Not the least of these from my perspective is the way the members of the task force have worked together. Differences have most certainly arisen, and I've regarded with great satisfaction the ways people used what they learned in the mediation to work them through. At key moments, the group has recommitted itself to the fundamentals of consensus, remembering that each individual stood for the dignity of every point of view. People have spoken hard truths with kindness; at the hardest moments, affection has carried the day.

I've remained involved. Although I wished to pull back and cede control to community members, within a few months the task force asked me to help them through a hard moment. Once done—very easily, I might add—they strongly requested that I stay on, not as mediator but as facilitator. Inevitably, I've served in the dual role of participant-neighbor as well as facilitator. This question of what happens after the mediation is over is a puzzling one. My chosen work is diving into the thick of controversy; I've mostly stayed away from organizational consulting after the fact. But now and then I hear a compelling reason to stay involved. When people have a genuine desire to work inter-culturally, and when they recognize the need for ongoing learning in order to do so, then I see a role for my continued leadership. Also, in the Bernal case, I continued to act both as leader and as neighbor. From that close vantage point, I've enjoyed seeing how much each member of the task force has learned, with what heart and effectiveness everyone takes part.

What is harder to assess is the impact on the community as a whole. To me, a perfect result would have included our finding more ways to involve the larger community than we did. The work of organizing and producing the art has been all-consuming. Everyone involved, even our professional project manager, is engaged in busy other lives. A largely volunteer force can only do so much. To be sure, there has been a visible impact on the community. At one point, the process was delayed by some legal questions raised by a person who had not earlier been involved in the Bernal conflict, who in fact had no particular relationship to the community. He made some nasty charges about some of the officials who supported the project. Another man living in a nearby neighborhood was shocked at these allegations. So on an early Saturday morning, he decided to hang out near the Bernal library and ask people what they thought. He stopped many passersby at random. A couple of people had no opinion, but everyone else fully applauded what we were doing. Several said they had wanted no artwork on the walls, or that they mourned the loss of the original mural. But what superseded those opinions, they said, was their pride in how the community had handled the conflict. Hearing of this surprise survey, we who had worked so hard on the process were enormously heartened.

I've never liked the word "intractability." I'm an idealist, no doubt, but I do think that we can make progress in most places where conflict seems entrenched if we have the courage, the wisdom, and the honesty to look beneath the surface and face the heart of the matter. Often, intractability is another word for felt helplessness, and often we feel helpless when we know in our hearts that the real issues are about injustice. If we could truly challenge economic violence and all other sorts of oppression, no conflict would be intractable. If the Bernal mediation is a small example of that truth, then I hope it also serves as a large encouragement to keep doing the good work toward making a socially just world.

Cast of Characters

Methods and Tools

Chronology

Appendixes

Works Cited

Index

. . .

# Cast of Characters

**Participants in the Mediation**

*Susan Kelk Cervantes*, a Caucasian woman, founding director of Precita Eyes Muralists, a long-established Bernal Heights nonprofit dedicated to community mural art around the Bay Area and beyond

*Larry Cruz*, a gay Latino homeowner and member of the board of the Bernal Heights Neighborhood Center, but taking part as an individual; a retired public servant who served in a variety of positions, including as aide to a San Francisco mayor

*Monique Jaquez*, a young Latina, third generation on the hill, an artist employed at Darcy's store; she was concerned that changing demographics of the community be reflected in the artwork

*Darcy Lee*, a white woman, store owner on Cortland Avenue and president of the Bernal Business Alliance

*Dan Martinez*, a Latino printer, young father, active parishioner in a Catholic church on Cortland Avenue; he was a member of the Save the Bernal Library Mural committee and was proposed by Mauricio

*Terry Milne*, a white man, longtime resident on the hill, an artist, author, and historian

*Brandon Powell*, a relative newcomer and the African-American father of young children in an interracial family; he favored preserving what could be saved of the mural

*Michael Smith*, also a young African-American father and a member of one of the design review committees on the hill; he identified himself as an historic preservationist and could also "see the other side"

*Giulio Sorro*, a young biracial high school teacher, the son of well-known activists; grew up on the hill and still living there

*Amy Trachtenberg*, a white woman mentioned often by others as respected and influential; a visual artist who had recently completed an elaborate library project in a nearby city; she expressed a wish that the Bernal mural not be restored, and was open to creative alternatives

*Mauricio Vela*, a Latino activist, organizer of the Save the Bernal Mural movement; a past executive director of the Bernal Heights Neighborhood Center

*Johanna Silva Waki*, a Latina woman, her family having lived for several generations on the hill, representing the board of the Neighborhood Center as its chair

## City Officials

*David Campos*, the representative from Bernal to the city-wide Board of Supervisors; the sponsor of the mediation

*Luis Herrera*, the city librarian

# Methods and Tools

What follows is intended to be a checklist of skills and strategies paralleling the narrative in Part One:

1. The Context: Exploring the Terrain
The work starts with a series of questions for the mediator:
* *Am I the right person for the job?*
    > Am I a good cultural fit?
    > Should I be working with a partner who broadens our understanding of the cultures represented?
    > Does this project confront me with particular challenges to my relationships with people taking part, or with people not directly involved but present in my own life?
* *Who needs to take part for the work to succeed?*
    > Who are the obvious participants? Examples: the divorcing couple, people who have spoken out on the subject, the principles to a contract.
    > Who exercises important influence on the conflict but isn't a primary party to it? Examples: new partners of the divorcing couple, people who have not spoken out publicly but are impacted by the outcome, subcontractors, and agents. It helps to think outside the professional box, to imagine whose presence might influence the process either positively or negatively, i.e., who might support a positive outcome with needed information, emotional nurturing, assistance with implementation of agreements, etc.? Alternatively, who might have unnoticed sway over agreements made in mediation, who therefore needs to be involved?
    > How much time is realistically needed to do a good job? For example, with two people involved I never mediate for fewer than

three hours. As the number of participants increases, so should the time to ensure everyone has a chance to speak fully and to enter into the negotiations without undue pressure.

2. The Setup: Composition and Design
This phase focuses on questions for the participants:
* *Finalize decisions* about who will take part
* When possible, *connect with each participant* to answer questions, hear background information, and establish rapport
* Make all *physical arrangements* clearly
  > Where will you meet?
  > If you'll meet longer than half a day, what are the provisions for food?
  > How much are your fees? When and how can they be paid? Example: I charge on a sliding scale; it is subjective, which means that people make their own decisions about what they can afford. I urge people to share the costs, to split the time, and to pay whatever they can afford for their portion of the time.
* Coach participants to *prepare*
  > What questions do you want participants to have thought about?
  > What emotional preparation do they need? Example: I ask people to prepare written notes, when possible, of what has upset them and what they want (more detail below).

3. The Beginning: Goals, Roles, and Power Relations
Once participants are gathered for the face-to-face work, the mediator's work includes teaching tools and helping participants practice them:
* Tools
  > "Held Feelings" (or "Stamps")
    - The speaker (address an individual by name; in a group larger than two, ask whether the person addressed is ready to listen): "When you did/said/didn't do [describe an action], I felt [name emotions]."
    - The listener: take note but don't respond (except perhaps to ask for additional information if needed to locate the incident in the listener's memory)
    - Later, a decision can be made whether the content needs to be discussed.

> *Paranoias* (or checking out assumptions and intuition)
>    ▪ The speaker: "I have the [*paranoia*/intuition/fear/concern] that you [think/feel/want] [a story of what the speaker imagines is going on for the listener].
>    ▪ The listener:
>       • "The kernel of truth is [validation]."
>       • "What is not true is [reassurance/correction/new information]."

* Power analysis: power is a process taking place in several domains simultaneously, all intertwined:
   > Internal
   > Interpersonal
   > Organizational
   > Cultural
   > Social Structural

4. Storytelling: Emotion and Meaning

Feelings are not irrational; they always make sense within a particular framework of understanding. Making sense of feelings is therefore a central goal of emotional discourse in mediation. The process of analyzing emotion requires tools for constructing frameworks that bring disparate perspectives and feelings into a common narrative. To create these analytic stories is to make meaning of their stories in ways that allow people to forgive each other and themselves.

5. Analysis: Getting to the Heart of the Matter

Some tools for creating analytic frameworks are:
   ▪ Nested theory: placing a particular dispute in wider and wider contexts of relationship and social structures lends dignity to people's conflict behaviors
      • How are people present in the dispute connected to others who don't appear overtly in the conflict?
      • What day-to-day interactions influence participants' conflict behaviors and positions? Contacts with neighbors, shopkeepers, relatives?
      • What web of obligations, identifications, or commitments are influencing the views of the participants?

- Power theory: naming the many realms in which power is operating in the conflict allows people to see their own role in the dynamics of fighting.
- Distinguishing interests and positions: going more deeply into the reasons why people want what they want creates options.
- Decoding culture: identifying cultural worldviews that give rise to different perspectives and understandings opens avenues for respect for different behaviors. Risk asking directly, "Because we come from differing cultural backgrounds, are you willing to help me by telling me whatever I need to know about your cultural framework?"
    - How are differences in communication approaches showing up in the dialogue?
    - What assumptions underlie persistent emotions? Is the framework individualist or collectivist, for instance? Do people think in terms of "me" or "us"?
    - What values do different participants hold constant? Is loyalty to an identity group, family, organization more important than self-interest?
    - Which rights do people believe to be primary: Autonomy? Freedom of choice? Support by the state or community?

6. Negotiation: Swings and Crunches
* *Consensus Decision-Making Process*
    > Ask for 100 percent of what you want: no more, no less
    > Expansively describe underlying interests
    > Check for areas of preexisting agreement
    > Identify specific issues to negotiate
    > Continue to negotiate until everyone is in sufficient agreement to proceed
* *Negotiate from the Ideal*
    > Identify expanded resources
    > Dream new possibilities (including consulting more people for ideas)
    > Look for equal compromises
    > Offer compensation for greater compromises
    > State agreement clearly
    > Check resolution against reality

> Commit to cooperative revisions rather than unilateral noncompliance

8. Consensus! . . . and Disruption

Having reached an agreement, both mediators and mediatees may be ready to end the work. Fatigue and relief can combine with the result that an important step is overlooked: nailing down the details.

* Ask questions about implementation:
    > What is the agreement that's just been made?
    > What needs to be done to implement it?
    > Who is going to do what actions to make it happen?
* Attend with practicality and compassion to the needs of each person:
    > What insight can the mediator share about obstacles each person may need to overcome?
    > What kinds of support and resources does each participant need in order to accomplish what s/he is committing to do?
* Construct a "safety net":
    > How will each person know that the actions are actually happening? (Some people call this step "accountability," but I tend to steer away from this word because it can assume a moral edge that leads to judgment of self and others.)
    > What will they do to renegotiate if implementation turns out not to happen?
* Strokes:
    > Ending with the positive is a crucial final step. Some characteristics of powerful strokes:
        * They are concrete.
        * They speak to who the recipient is more than to what she or he has done.
        * They focus on the recipient, not the giver: i.e., strokes in the form of "I love you because you take such good care of me" may be heard as an injunction rather than a recognition.
        * They avoid comparisons: "You are the best cook in the world. I could never cook so well" requires the recipient to agree to the put-down of the giver—and of everyone else who cooks.
        * They are fun!
    > How you know that a stroke has been received:

- The recipient smiles!
- The recipient may say "Thank you" but does not immediately minimize the stroke ("You look beautiful in that shirt." "Oh this old thing? I found it in the back of my closet.") or immediately return the stroke ("You look good, too.")

9. Aftermath: Into the Community, Onto the Walls

Every mediation takes place in a particular social context; therefore, what has just happened in the room is tested and changed by engagement with other concerned people who have not been present. It often is helpful to have detailed agreements about how the participants will talk about the work.

# Chronology

| DATE | ACTIVITY | LOCATION | FOCUS | OUTSIDE EVENTS |
|------|----------|----------|-------|----------------|
| 1/23/10 | First session | Library | Positions | |
| 1/25 | | | | Mauricio's Facebook page |
| 1/26 | Second session | Larry's | Interest | |
| 1/27 | | | | "Save" posters along Cortland |
| 1/30 | | | | Library reopens Small groups |
| 2/6 | Third session | Bernal Heights Neighborhood Center (BHNC) | Negotiation | |
| 2/13 | | | | Darcy's Facebook page |
| 2/16 | | | Draft consensus statement | |
| 2/16 | | | | Meeting with directors of library and arts commissions, Supervisor Campos, et al. |
| 2/17 | | | | Meeting with Ellen, Lisa, Darcy, Roseanne |

| DATE | ACTIVITY | LOCATION | FOCUS | OUTSIDE EVENTS |
|------|----------|----------|-------|----------------|
| 2/24 | Fourth session | BHNC | Negotiation | |
| 3/1 | Committee | | Revise statement | |
| 3/2 | | | | Andover wall mural painted over |
| 3/16 | | | | Billboard |
| 3/17 | Fifth session | BHNC | Consensus | |
| 3/18 | | | | Amy's and others' second thoughts |
| 3/28 | Sixth session | | Final version | |
| 3/31 | | | Revised consensus | |
| 4/1 | | | | Meeting with David and two commission directors |
| 4/26 | Community meeting | | | |

# APPENDIX A

# Preparation for First Session

January 16, 2010

From: Beth Roy

To:     Bernal Library mural mediatees

*Re:     Welcome & preparation for the mediation*

Many thanks to all of you for the stimulating and passionate conversations we've been having. Bernal Heights so contradicts the current notion that we're "bowling alone." This is a community of engaged and dedicated people!

We're on for a mediation:

SATURDAY, JANUARY 23, 10 AM TO 2 PM,
AT THE BERNAL LIBRARY

We're still finalizing the list of participants and will distribute it before we meet. We'll be 8 to 10 people. I'll be working with a wonderful colleague of mine: Cynthia Luna. She lives in southern California, comes from Mexico City, where she currently does a portion of her ongoing work on leadership in corporate and community settings. Cynthia has trained with me and is wise and talented; I feel enormously happy to have her participation in this project. Larry Cruz has consulted with me from the start of planning the mediation, giving me important insight and support. He'll take part in the mediation as well.

We'd like you to do some work in preparation for the session—a series of notes on your thoughts and feelings. Bring the notes to the session—for your eyes only. We've found that using the space before a mediation to sort through what you want to say is a very helpful tool in making the face-to-face work effective.

1. *Goals for the mediation*: What are you hoping the mediation will accomplish? Some examples might be:

- Some things that have happened in the course of this conflict have left me hurt and wary. I'd like to clear the air.
- I want to keep the decision about the mural within the community, and so I'd like to think creatively with people here about solutions that would satisfy us all.

2. *Emotional wounds*: We recommend a way to think about expressing feelings that aims to be both respectful and honest. It consists of a two-part sentence. The first part describes the action that evoked your feelings, and the second part names the emotions you felt:

▪ When you did/said/wrote _____
(an action: words, gestures, acts, etc.),
▪ I felt _____ (an emotion: angry, hurt, sad, scared, etc.).

3. *Resolution*: What do you wish happens with the murals? We ask that you think about this question in two parts:

▪ First, if you could have perfection—no problems of funding, what you want goes!—what would that be?
▪ Next, if you knew that the decision had already been made elsewhere to do something other than what you want, what are at least 2 alternatives that would please you?

4. *Appreciation*: What recognition—genuine compliments and gratitude, nothing contrived, please!—would you like to give to others who have been involved in this controversy? Some questions to consider:

- What do you appreciate about individuals present in the room?
- What do you appreciate about this community?
- What gifts do you bring to the table and to the community?

If you need any help preparing, or have any questions before we meet, don't hesitate to get in touch.

We see this process as an opportunity to continue the Bernal tradition of creating community in a mold that is conscious, participatory, and respectful. It is also a means to turn a significant conflict, with deep feeling and much dignity on all sides, into a creative step toward something new and wonderful. We are very grateful to you all for taking part, and look forward eagerly to the 23rd.

Beth Roy
Cynthia Luna

# APPENDIX B

# Preparation for Second Session

You all are a great group to mediate! I think we made very good progress on Saturday, so I'm eager to move forward Tuesday evening. Larry has very generously offered his house for the meeting. He'd like you to be forewarned that he has a dog—and I can testify that she's a large friendly honey of a dog. If that's a problem, let us know and we'll tend to it. To remind you, we decided to meet from 7:30 to 10 pm.

Here are some things I'd like to urge you to think about (make notes about, if you have the will):

> Cynthia urged you to "walk in the other's shoes." Will you concretize that by seeing if you can summarize the positions and the interests you heard expressed by others? One way to think about the difference between positions and interests:
  - A position is what you want.
  - Interests are the reasons why you want it.
> Be prepared to name the most important qualities you want in the community in which you live.
> Be prepared to list the qualities you heard from other people, and note where they concur and differ from your own.

The provisional agenda is:

1. Tend to some questions and hanging threads from Saturday's session.
2. Clarify positions and interests.
3. Define the process by which we'll move forward (I'll do some teaching about consensus and other elements).
4. Engage in building consensus.
5. Take stock and plan next steps.
6. End with acknowledgements.

If you have any questions, or anything else you'd like to put in the mix for the next meeting, don't hesitate to be in touch.

Beth Roy

# APPENDIX C

# First Draft of Consensus Statement

Proposal (to test consensus)

## WHAT WE PROPOSE DOING:
## UPDATING THE MURAL

> Inaugurate a new community project at the Bernal library to produce an updated mural in accordance with the following principles and priorities:

- The work gives voice to marginalized segments of the community, especially youth and seniors.
- The work honors the history and meanings of both the existing mural and also the WAP building, telling the story of both in its portrayal of the history of the community, a history that has evolved to include newcomers with diverse lifestyles.
- The work is visually pleasing to the many cultural sensibilities within the community.
- The work embraces a variety of sites on and around the library building as well as new media and forms.

## PRESERVING THE ORIGINAL MURAL

> Images of the existing mural in its original form will be put on permanent display inside the library, along with text explaining the meanings of the visual elements.

## HOW WE PROPOSE TO DO IT:
## COMMUNITY PROCESS

> The intention of the mural process is to contribute to greater understanding and cooperation among diverse members of the multicultural, multi-class Bernal community. Therefore, under the leadership of experienced community artists, decisions will be made by consensus

through a respectful, patient, and creative effort to embrace the visions of all participants.

## QUALITIES AND VALUES

> In the end, the mural will visually recount history with emotional integrity, promote a vision of social justice on the hill and in the world, and bring to the library campus images of beauty that invite the fullest and most joyous uses of the library itself.

# APPENDIX D

# Mediation Group's Statement
# about the Andover Mural

March 11, 2010

To the Bernal Community:

We are writing this statement in response to the loss in early March of the Andover Street retaining wall mural (alongside the library and recreation center).

We are residents of Bernal Heights who have been participating in mediated sessions to find a solution to the controversy surrounding the mural on our branch library. We came together at the request of Supervisor David Campos and under the leadership of Bernal-ite Beth Roy, an experienced mediator. With a commitment to honest, respectful interaction, we have talked deeply about the meanings and emotions associated with both the mural's images and the origins of the building in the depression-era WPA program. We've been moved by each other's stories, clearing up some hard feelings and opening up space for collaborative, creative thinking. We are now very close to agreement to extend a proposal to the larger community.

The mural on the walls of the library is separate from the mural on the Andover retaining wall. Our work concerns the library mural, not the Andover mural. Nonetheless, when the Andover mural was painted out, strong feelings and concerns were raised that relate to community art in general. Josef Norris, the artist who created the Andover mural, chose to paint it out without consultation within the community. The reasons he has voiced concern deterioration of the wall and therefore of the mural images, the expense in both time and material required to restore the painting, and Josef's feelings of dismay as he saw portraits of the many Bernal citizens represented in the work deteriorate. In the belief that he owned the right to do with the work what he wished, he chose to eliminate it.

The lack of shared process could not contrast more sharply with the process our group has undertaken, reflecting a very different approach to both community relations and community art. We believe that all art in public spaces is an endeavor shared between artists and the people in whose midst the work exists. It symbolizes values and aesthetics that can be a progressive force, and also a source of controversy. Ownership becomes a complex concept; it may literally belong to the artist whose hand held the brush, but it has meanings that create a different sort of ownership for those who walk past it on a daily basis—especially when the work is designed and, perhaps, executed with substantial community involvement.

We wish to share with our neighbors our sense of grief and anger that the Andover mural is gone and the manner in which it was removed. We also wish to initiate a process of collaborative art-making on and around the library that respects the meanings and sensibilities of all Bernal residents. We'll be releasing our consensus statement very soon with a concrete proposal to that end.

Susan Cervantes, Larry Cruz, Monique Jaquez, Darcy Lee, Dan Martinez, Terry Milne, Brandon Powell, Beth Roy, Johanna Silva Waki, Michael Smith, Guilio Sorro, Amy Trachtenberg

# APPENDIX E

# Final Consensus Statement

STATEMENT OF CONSENSUS

Bernal Heights Library Mural Mediation

Beginning in January of this year, a group of residents of Bernal Heights participated in mediation to seek resolution to controversies surrounding the mural on the walls of the Bernal branch library. The mediation was sponsored by Supervisor David Campos and led by Bernal resident Beth Roy. With a shared commitment to principles of equity and justice, and through a process of deep dialogue, exploration of meanings, and respectful relationship building, the group produced the following recommendations:

PRINCIPLES OF AGREEMENT: BERNAL LIBRARY ARTWORK

The Bernal community is committed to progressive principles of inclusion, social justice, and creativity.

*The Bernal library mural is meaningful to many members of the community:*
> It exemplifies respect for people with deep roots on the hill, especially for those whose lifestyles have been altered by economic forces changing housing patterns over recent decades.
> It is a legacy of Arch Williams, a pioneer of the San Francisco mural movement.
> It represents the long reach of Bernal's history, from Native American occupants to the early 1980s when it was created.

*The Bernal library building is a significant landmark in the community:*
> Its architecture is aesthetically excellent.
> It was built as part of the WPA program of the 1930s, a tribute to the principle of collective responsibility during hard times and to the ability of responsive government to promote creativity, beauty, and support for the public good.

> The renovation of the interior exemplifies a lush and inviting presence for the many programs and resources offered by the library.

In an effort to honor all these principles, we offer a resolution to the mural dispute, arrived at through a process of consensus that itself manifests the principles of respect and equity we hold in common.

## WHAT WE PROPOSE DOING: REVITALIZING
## THE ARTWORK ON THE LIBRARY

Inaugurate a new art project at the Bernal library, to produce a contemporary art work in accordance with the following priorities:

1. Themes of social justice and representing the whole community will continue to be central to the artwork. The artwork will give voice to and be representative of the whole community.

2. The artwork will honor and build on the history, meanings and content of both the existing mural and also the WPA building, evoking the story of both in its reflection of the history of the community, a history that has evolved to include newcomers with diverse lifestyles. Specific elements of the existing mural have importance for members of the community; the chosen artistic team will be involved in identifying, retaining and reflecting those images in the new art work with the input of the community.

3. The artwork will be designed and led by a diverse team of artists selected by a task force formed from among the mediation group in consultation with Bernal residents with needed expertise. Criteria for selection will be developed by the task force and will include the following: the chosen artists should represent a wide range of experiences in public and community-based art development. Priority will be given to Bernal artists. The process will be inclusive and collaborative.

4. The artwork will be designed so as to respect the lines and intentions of the architecture, creating balance between artwork and façade. The entire area within the property lines of the library will be considered for free-standing or mural or integrated artwork. The artwork will engage the site and building on the south, east, and north sides as determined by the selected artist team after meetings and other processes with the community processes have taken place.

5. The new artwork will use media that requires little or no maintenance, such as painted tile, mosaic, metalwork, ceramics or other permanent mediums.

6. No existing artwork will be removed or painted over until the funding and design processes are in place.

## PRESERVING THE ORIGINAL MURAL

Images of the existing mural in its original form will be put on permanent display inside the library, along with text explaining the meanings of the visual elements and, through the story of the making of the mural, does honor to Arch Williams.

## HOW WE PROPOSE TO DO IT: COMMUNITY PROCESS

The intention of the mural process is to contribute to greater understanding and cooperation among diverse members of the multicultural, multi-class Bernal community.

## QUALITIES AND VALUES

In the words of a mediation participant: "We have an opportunity to create a significant event in the neighborhood. When the library was built, that was a significant event. When the mural was painted, that was a significant event. This is the time for a third significant event, revitalizing the Library building. Fifty years from now, people in the community will look at what we do today and honor it."

In the end, the artwork will respond with emotional integrity and a sense of memory and history, promote a vision of social justice on the hill and in the world, and bring to the library campus images of beauty that invite the fullest and most joyous uses of the library itself.

*Signed*: Susan Cervantes, Supervisor David Campos, Larry Cruz, Monique Jaquez, Darcy Lee, Dan Martinez, Terry Milne, Ellen Morrison, Brandon Powell, Beth Roy, Michael Smith, Johanna Silva Waki, Guilio Sorro, Amy Trachtenberg, Mauricio Vela
March 28, 2010

# Works Cited

Birkhoff, Juliana. 2000. *Mediators' Perspectives on Power: A Window into a Profession*. Unpublished dissertation, George Mason University.

Burdick, John, Louis Kriesberg, and Beth Roy. 2010. "A Conversation between Conflict Resolution and Social Movement Scholars." *Conflict Resolution Quarterly* 27 (4): 347–68.

Bush, Robert A. Baruch, and Joseph P. Folger. 1994. *The Promise of Mediation: Responding to Conflict through Empowerment and Recognition*. San Francisco: Jossey-Bass.

Chené, Roberto. 2008. "Beyond Mediation—Reconciling an Intercultural World." In *Re-Centering Culture and Knowledge in Conflict Resolution Practice*, edited by Mary Adams Trujillo, S. Y. Bowland, Linda James Myers, Phillip M. Richards, and Beth Roy. Syracuse, NY: Syracuse University Press.

Cobb, Sarah. 2001. "Liminal Spaces in Negotiation Processes: Crossing Relational Boundaries and Interpretative Thresholds in a Family Business Negotiation." Presented to Psychoanalysis and Negotiation Seminar, Program on Negotiation, Harvard Law School, Cambridge, MA, November.

Dugan, Maire. 1996. "A Nested Theory of Conflict." *Women in Leadership* 1 (Summer): 9–20.

Fisher, Roger, and William Ury. 1981. *Getting to Yes: Negotiating Agreement without Giving In*. New York: Houghton Mifflin.

Gramsci, Antonio. 1997. *Selections from the Prison Notebooks*. Edited and translated by Quintin Hoare and Geoffrey Nowell Smith. New York: International Publishers.

Institute for Women's Policy Research (IWPR). 2011. "Access to Paid Sick Days Less Common Among Workers of Color." (March 15, 2011) http://www.iwpr.org/press-room/press-releases/access-to-paid-sick -days-less-common-among-workers-of-color.

Jones, Carolyn. 2012. "Ex-Criminal Tries to Bring Peace to Oakland Streets." *San Francisco Chronicle*, December 26, 1.

Kolb, Deborah M., and Associates. 1997. *When Talk Works: Profiles of Mediators*. San Francisco: Jossey-Bass.

Lederach, John Paul. 1997. *Building Peace: Sustainable Reconciliation in Divided Societies*. Washington, DC: United States Institute of Peace.

Nader, Laura. 1988. "The ADR Explosion—The Implications of Rhetoric in Legal Reform." *Windsor Yearbook of Access to Justice* 8:269–91.

Roy, Beth. 1994. *Some Trouble with Cows: Making Sense of Social Conflict*. Berkeley: University of California Press.

Roy, Beth. 1999. *Bitters in the Honey: Tales of Hope and Disappointment across Divides of Race and Time*. Fayetteville: University of Arkansas Press.

Roy, Beth. 2007. "Radical Psychiatry: Therapeutic Change for Self and Society." In *Advancing Social Justice through Clinical Practice*, edited by Etiony Aldarondo. New York: Routledge.

Scott, James. 1992. *Domination and the Arts of Resistance: Hidden Transcripts*. New Haven, CT: Yale University Press.

Steiner, Claude. 1981. *The Other Side of Power*. New York: Grove.

Steiner, Claude. 2009. *The Heart of the Matter*. Pleasanton, CA: TA Press.

Wyckoff, Hogie. 1980. *Solving Problems Together*. New York: Grove.

# Index